COMPLETING LUTHER'S REFORMATION

COMPLETING LUTHER'S REFORMATION

David Pawson

Anchor Recordings

Copyright © 2017 David Pawson

The right of David Pawson to be identified as author of this Work has been asserted by him in accordance with the Copyright, Designs and Patents Act 1988.

First published in Great Britain in 2017 by
Anchor Recordings Ltd
DPTT, Synegis House, 21 Crockhamwell Road,
Woodley, Reading RG5 3LE

No part of this publication may be reproduced or transmitted in any form or by any means, electronic or mechanical, including photocopy, recording or any information storage and retrieval system, without prior permission in writing from the publisher.

**For more of David Pawson's teaching,
including DVDs and CDs, go to
www.davidpawson.com**

**FOR FREE DOWNLOADS
www.davidpawson.org**

**For further information, email
info@davidpawsonministry.org**

ISBN 978-1-911173-26-7

Printed by LightningSource

Contents

Preface	6
Revival or Reformation?	7
Church and State	33
Ministry Matters	53
Tying up Loose Ends	77

This book is based on a series of talks. Originating as it does from the spoken word, its style will be found by many readers to be somewhat different from my usual written style. It is hoped that this will not detract from the substance of the biblical teaching found here.

As always, I ask the reader to compare everything I say or write with what is written in the Bible and, if at any point a conflict is found, always to rely upon the clear teaching of scripture.

David Pawson

REVIVAL OR REFORMATION?

My subject, *Completing Luther's Reformation for the Twenty-first Century*, came to me at a time when Scandinavia was on my heart, with visits to Finland and Norway, when I was asking, "What is the greatest need of the Church in Scandinavia?" There are two possible answers to that. One answer is "revival" and the other is "reformation". Now this raises a fundamental question: in countries where the Church is in decline, what are we going to pray for and what are we going to do about this? I find that Christians divide into two main groups: those who are waiting for God to do something about it and those who believe God is waiting for *us* to do something about it. Here are two quite different approaches to the present situation, born out of despair in some sense, when we look at the declining influence we have on society. I want to declare my position right from the beginning. I am on the *reformation* side. I believe that God is waiting for *us* to do things. That may or may not lead to revival. The two could be related, but if they are, then I believe reformation is the priority.

I was at a prayer meeting for revival in England. For three hours, people prayed for God to do something. Then suddenly, a young teenage boy stood up and gave a prophecy. I shall never forget it. In a penetrating voice, this shy boy—

I found out later that he was quite retiring, not the sort who would get up, raise his voice and correct his elders — just got up and said, "Thus says the Lord: 'I will not revive what I never built,'" and he sat down. It transformed the entire prayer meeting; it came with such authority in the Spirit. That word came ringing through. We realised we were really asking God to revive what *we* had built.

God was telling us that he would not revive what he never built and I cannot help but believe that while the Church is deliberately disobeying the commandments of the Lord, and has compromised in so many areas, there is no reason why he should answer prayers to revive it. That is my problem. The state of our nation is due to the state of the Church and we must take responsibility for what is happening around us. We are to be the salt and light but we need to acknowledge that we have not lived up to this ideal, and that we have compromised on the Word of God in so many ways already that it is almost impudence to ask the Lord to revive us.

That is where I am coming from, and my words apply especially to countries which have a State church. I refer, therefore, to most of northern Europe. We have a Church of England, which is losing one thousand people a week. That is a hemorrhage that the Church cannot afford. It is not just the loss of quantity of membership, but the loss of quality. In Britain, as in Norway, we are in much the same sort of crisis about homosexual marriage, about all kinds of ways in which the Church is, alas, instead of leading society up the hill, following society down the hill, only about fifteen years later. So, we are seen as people who are dragging our heels and following the world and gradually accepting the world's standards after they have already accepted them themselves. We should be leading up the hill and saying, "This is the way to a healthy, happy, holy society; come with us," but we seem to be doing the exact opposite. I believe

God is deeply grieved by this.

The Church of England of course, unlike the State Church in Norway, was born in adultery and murder. The foundation has been cracked from the very beginning. It is no coincidence that a church born in the adultery of the king, Henry VIII, is now facing gender and sexual issues which could tear it apart. The cracks were there from the beginning and were never really repented of or acknowledged. But that is my situation in England. In Norway, the State church was born out of Martin Luther's Reformation, whether directly or indirectly. I know he never went to Norway, but his ideas certainly did.

Luther rediscovered one major answer to the question, "How does the Head in heaven communicate with the Body on earth?" Or to put it another way, "How does the Head in heaven control the Body on earth?" I believe the Church is in a spastic condition, in which the Body is no longer responding as it should to the Head's direction.

In Australia, I spoke by invitation to six hundred clergy of the Uniting Church at their synod in a theatre. I tackled this question there. I said, "There are two ways in which the head of the Church communicates to his body and controls his body. One is scripture and the other is the Spirit. These are his means of communicating his will to us. If we ignore those two ways of his communication — the scripture, which has come to us from his past revelation, and the Spirit communicating his present— then we have a problem. I have sat in on your synod for the whole morning session, when you have discussed whether to ordain practising, homosexual pastors to your church; in the whole debate, for three hours, I never heard the scripture quoted, and I never heard the Spirit mentioned. You are a spastic body. You are doing your own thing."

Well, I was not prepared for the response. They leapt to

their feet; they yelled at me. They shook their fists at me, and I simply walked quietly through them and out of the theatre. It was quite a thing. It hit the headlines of the press, I'm afraid. But there is no harm in bad publicity. Actually, there is no such thing as bad publicity. I am not a person who "walks around the porridge," I walk into it wherever I go! But years ago, I took a vow to the Lord. I said, "Lord, here's a mouth, and whatever you tell me to say I will say, whatever the cost or consequence." I meant it.

By the grace of God, I have been able to keep that vow and promise. It is not the way to be a popular preacher, though it is the way to be a well-known one! But there we are; that's me. I believe the Lord is looking for men and women who will open their mouths and tell the truth, the whole truth, and nothing but the truth, as it is, without fear of man or fear of woman. That can be greater sometimes, I have discovered, with pastors and pastors' wives.

Luther discovered one of the ways in which the head communicates with the body: scripture. His principle was: scripture alone (*sola scriptura*). That is the principle that I want to commend to you. When he said, "My conscience is captive to the Word of God. Here I stand; I can do no other," that was equivalent to the vow I took years ago, that I would study the Bible as hard as I could. I would read as many contrary interpretations as I could get hold of, so I would listen to others. But when I came to a final conclusion myself about what the Bible taught, I would teach it, whatever it cost. And it has cost. Nevertheless, that is where I stand. I believe I am standing with Luther there.

It was on that ground that he swept away many centuries-old traditions of the Church in which he was brought up. He swept away relics, pilgrimages, purgatory, indulgences, five of the seven sacraments; he was willing to bring the sole test of scripture to all these areas and was bold enough to deal with them. That kind of courage is desperately needed in the Church today. But I find there are few voices that are willing to tell it as it is. Most pastors admit to me freely that they have compromised and know it. But the fear of losing members, when your church is already shrinking, is a kind of syndrome that is difficult to resist.

Luther, therefore, put scripture above tradition. I believe that is the call now in our times. For we have traditions that may go back only to the Reformation, and they are only three or four hundred years old, yet they too need to be brought under the test of scripture. Whether we are as willing, as Luther was, to do that in our day is the real test of our obedience to the Lord.

Now my thesis is this: Luther did not complete the Reformation. He did not consistently apply that principle to all that he inherited from the medieval Church. The call today is to complete what he began. To some people, I have found that is almost heresy. To suggest that Luther didn't have the last word on anything, and that he might not have completed what he began is thought to be heresy. But I am going to show you ten areas in which he failed to apply the principle of scripture. Five of them are concerned with what we preach and the other five are linked with how we build the Church. I believe that these ten areas are ones in which, today, we need to be reformers according to the Word of God, as he was, and to be as bold as he was.

He didn't have to pay the supreme price, but I am a great admirer of Jan Hus, who a hundred years before Luther did what Luther did, but paid the price of being burned alive at the stake in Constance. In Prague he began a reformation which later was crushed by Catholic armies, fighting those who became known as the "Hussites". I have this interest because my son-in-law is Czech, and he and my daughter bought an abandoned hotel in the town where Hus was, right next door to the Hus Museum. The hotel was renovated and the President of the Czech Republic has stayed there.

I got a real interest through that link with Jan Hus and have become a great fan of him because he was willing to pay the price, and he paid it severely. He was promised by the Holy Roman Emperor safe conduct to his trial, where they found him guilty of heresy and burned him at the stake. When he appealed to the Emperor, "You promised me safe conduct if I would come to trial," the reply was, "I've promised you safe conduct there, but not safe conduct home again." That is how he was killed for his reformation.

Now Luther was not comfortable with the whole Bible; that was one of the roots of his inconsistency and failure to see it through. He majored, as you know, on Paul's writings. He was not comfortable with James, for reasons we will go into later. He called it an "epistle of straw". He was also very uncomfortable with the book of Revelation and, indeed, expressed the opinion that it shouldn't be in the Bible at all. He therefore handicapped the Church in its eschatology and in its hope for the future. But again, I will come to that in more detail. So, the first limitation on Luther was that he was not comfortable with the whole of scripture. Therefore, the principle "scripture alone" was compromised from the beginning. He failed to get the balance of the whole Bible, or even the whole New Testament.

The second failure, which came from that, was his failure to apply scripture to every part of the Christian life and the church life of his day. There were areas that he did not touch. I believe that God is calling us now (and I will give you the grounds for believing that) to complete that Reformation and take the whole scripture and apply it to the whole Christian life, the whole of our preaching and the whole of our Church structure.

I will begin, therefore, with a positive contribution: the

great discovery or rediscovery that he made, and which has affected all Protestant churches ever since and, indirectly, the Catholic Church, was justification by faith. That, I gauge, will of course be what he will be remembered for until Christ returns. That was his great contribution. It was the answer to the most fundamental question: how can I, as a human being, get into a right relationship with God since he is righteous and I am certainly not, by his standards anyway? That is the basic question. To put it another way, "What must I do to be saved?" Or to put it even more simply, "How do I become a Christian?" His answer was in that rediscovery of the doctrine of justification by faith – that God is willing to declare me righteous, to dismiss my case as innocent, which of course for a righteous God would be a totally unrighteous act. For a righteous God to *overlook* sin and offer to forget it would be impossible.

I was on British television just after the tsunami, answering the question, "Why does God allow natural disasters?" Among other things I said, "It is impossible for God to forgive sin." I paused; gave it a long pause. One lady wrote to me afterwards and said, "David Pawson's finally gone over the top. He's finally gone mental or crazy." But after the pause, I just said, "Until it's been paid for." At that addition, this lady said she burst into tears and wept for joy and thanked the Lord. A righteous God cannot forgive sin until it has been paid for. That is the truth that Martin Luther really discovered: that God can treat us as righteous, as if we had never sinned, but only on the ground of the death of Jesus Christ and his atoning work.

Now that was the major truth that Luther discovered. But he tended to make this the basic understanding of salvation. He made it not the beginning of salvation, but the middle and the end, so that this became all that was needed to get to heaven. This has dogged the Protestant churches ever since. The over-emphasis on one doctrine will always badly affect the others because the whole of Christian salvation, the whole doctrine of the gospel, depends on a number of features which interlock. When you put too much emphasis on one of them it throws the others out of balance. I believe that is what happened.

Luther was not the pope and would be horrified to be thought of as that, but it is amazing how many people treat him as an infallible teacher. I once said to a Catholic priest, "The one thing I admire about the Catholic Church is that you only have one infallible teacher. We Protestants have hundreds, if not thousands, and we tend to follow a teacher and treat him as infallible."

By the way, please don't believe anything I say or write unless you can find it for yourself in your Bible. That is my safety. It means that people who find it in the Bible don't say, "Do you know what David Pawson teaches?" They say, "Do you know what the Bible says?" I want to produce people from my ministry who will quote the Bible and not a teacher, because you can play one teacher off against another so easily; it is a game, and I am not into it.

Let us look at three or four effects of such an over-emphasis on justification by faith and what it has done to some of the other vital doctrines in scripture, relating to salvation. In this chapter I am dealing with individual salvation (we will deal with Church issues later). But I am concerned now with what we preach as the gospel of salvation. The first major effect it had was to put the focus of our preaching on the death of Christ rather than the resurrection. This is such a fundamental point that we are almost too close to it to recognise what has happened.

Let us put it against a wider backcloth. In the Middle Ages, Catholicism was obsessed with the crucifixion. If you went into a Catholic church you would see little or nothing but a dead Jesus. You would see the fourteen Stations of the Cross around the wall. You would see a big crucifix with Christ dead and hanging on it. The only depiction of a live person you would probably see would be a statue of Mary, living, smiling and looking at you. While Jesus is a dead figure all around you, Mary is the living figure. It is little wonder that naïve Catholics pray to Mary – she was seen as alive; Jesus as dead: "Yes, he died for us, but he's dead whereas Mary is alive; let's pray to someone who's alive."

I taught in Finland, and of course that country is in a unique situation. It was invaded by the Swedes, who brought Lutheranism, and by the Russians who brought Orthodoxy. When I went there on a previous occasion, I said to my guide, "I'd like to go and see those two cathedrals, inside." He asked why. "Well," I said, "What I expect to see is death in one and life in the other. Western Christianity, since the big split in 1054, has diverged. The Western churches consistently focus their preaching and their worship on the cross, on the death, whereas Orthodox churches in the East focus on the resurrection."

Well, I got a shock when I went into the Lutheran cathedral. There was a huge oil painting above the altar (or do you call it a table?). It was a three-metre high painting of Christ as a corpse. Not just dying on the cross, but as a corpse lying at the foot of the cross—cold, grey, blue almost. Dead: looking so dead that I have never seen a painting like it. Then I went into the Orthodox church and I said, "And what I expect to see here are a whole lot of icons or paintings of Jesus alive and looking at people." But it was even better than that. The major icon in the middle was a huge painting of Christ ascending, and, as he ascended, looking down with love and compassion at the human race he was leaving. It is a terrific painting. By the way, a lady there gave me a typical Orthodox icon. But that is not a dying Christ; that is a living Christ. That is why on Easter Sunday in Moscow, everybody greets everybody else with the words, "Christ is risen!" The response comes readily from anybody, "He is risen indeed!" For them, Easter Sunday is the heart of the gospel, not Good Friday.

Now this has been a difference between the Eastern and the Western churches since 1054. Luther, in a sense, did not correct that, because we are justified by his death. So, the typical Western preacher and evangelist today will quote a verse, or misquote a verse, "We preach Christ and him crucified," which is a bad translation. The Greek says, "We preach Christ and him *having been* crucified," which changes the whole verse. We are preaching a living Christ who has been crucified. But the big thing is he is alive and he is not dead.

I think of verses elsewhere. Paul, in Romans for example, says, "Being justified by his blood, how much more will we be saved by his life." Now that is an emphasis I miss in Western preaching. "The cross, the cross, the cross, he died for you; he took your sins away" – it is all there, but I don't often hear the resurrection preached as the key to the gospel. If you study the apostolic preaching in Acts, the resurrection was at the heart of it. Yes, they mentioned his death. Right through to Revelation, "I saw a Lamb, looking as though it had been slain, standing by the throne." This is not a dead lamb. It is a lamb that has been slain and looks as if it has been, but is very much alive and standing at the right hand of God.

I just mention this because if our whole salvation is tied to justification, it will inevitably keep us at the cross. As Paul said, "If Christ be not raised, you are still in your sins." In other words, the cross can do nothing for you without the resurrection. Now that is strange thinking to so many westerners because, yes, as Protestants we may not have had crucifixes, but we still had the cross, even if it was empty. That was still the symbol of our faith in our gospel, and still is. But the preaching in Acts was centered on the resurrection, which of course really is the key to our faith, because if Christ didn't rise from the dead we have deceived ourselves and we are deceiving everybody else, and we should close every church tomorrow because it is based on the biggest fraud in history. Now that is the first area. It is a difference in emphasis, not a radical change. But I believe we want to be known as those who preach a risen Jesus and, I would add, ascended Jesus. Far too many people think "Jesus lives in my heart". They have been asked to invite Jesus into their heart; they have never been told he is at the right hand of the Father. If he wasn't there, nobody could be baptised in the Holy Spirit, because he never did that while he was down here. He couldn't. He had to go back and receive the promise from the Father before he could do that for anyone. We are utterly dependent on the ascended Christ for our salvation.

I am allergic to that horrible expression "the finished work of Christ on the cross". It was finished insofar as atonement was concerned, but it was not the finished work of Jesus by a long way. The resurrection, and the ascension, and the return of Christ are all part of our salvation. I am not saved yet; I am looking forward to being. I am on the way of salvation, and it is great to be on the way. We will come back to that in a moment. So, this is the first change of emphasis I think we need to make: that the resurrection, the living, ascended Christ, is the heart of our preaching, not the cross. Thank God that the cross is part of it, but he didn't finish the work of salvation on the cross. It has gone on a long way since then.

Next, I believe that in his anxiety to preach against justification by works, Luther reduced faith, and even repentance, to a passive attitude rather than a positive action. In both cases in my New Testament, repentance and faith are things that we do and things that are absolutely necessary for our salvation. Both are defined in the New Testament in terms of works, in terms of deeds, in terms of actions. Luther, I think was so anxious to kill any thought of justification by works, which is the impression the medieval Church had given to so many people—that he couldn't cope with, for example, James 2, where James says, "Faith without works is dead. It can't save."

Of course, there was a simple misunderstanding there — that when Paul used the word "works" and James used it, they were talking about the same thing. For the word "works" has many different meanings in scripture. The word "works" basically is actions, but Paul, in all his references, was referring to works of the *law*. James was not; he was referring to works of *faith*. Indeed, before that, the New Testament calls us to works of repentance. Both of these are active actions on the part of human beings, which make it possible for them to appropriate the work of Christ in salvation. This has been an emphasis ever since. We have a phobia now about works that cannot cope with the use of the word in any connection with salvation.

Let me just expand on that a bit. Repentance: John the Baptist was the first person in the New Testament to use that word. He emphasised: "Bring forth fruits worthy of repentance." They said, "What do you mean?" He then spelled it out in terms of action for them to take. He told them, "If you are defrauding anybody, get your money straightened out." He spelled out in practical detail what repentance is. It is something we do. It begins with a change of mind. It moves on from thought to word, when we confess our sins, but it reaches a climax in deed when we turn away from our sins and put wrong things right. So, there is a loss of any thought of repentance as being something we do, not in order to earn salvation or deserve it, but in order to receive it (my understanding of the New Testament).

Let me be very practical here. A young man came to see me some time ago on a motorbike with high handlebars and mirrors and looking like a porcupine. He wore a black leather jacket covered with brass studs. He rang my doorbell and I said, "Hello, Paul. What can I do for you?"

"I want to talk."

"Alright, come on in," I replied. He came in and squirmed into one of our armchairs, which still bears the marks of the brass studs. I asked, "What do you want to talk about, Paul?"

He said, "I want to be baptised."

"Do you know how we baptise people here?"

"Yeah, you dunk them in the water."

"So, you want me to dunk you in the water?"

"Yeah."

I said, "Paul, do you know what the word 'repent' means?"

"No; never heard it."

I said, "Well I want you to do something. Go home and ask Jesus one question: is there anything in my life that you don't like? When he answers, cut it out and come back."

Three weeks later he rang the front doorbell.

I said, "What is it, Paul?"

He said, "There."

"What do you mean?"

"I've stopped biting my nails."

"Alright, Paul, I'll baptise you now." I did and he has never looked back. He was proving his repentance to me; he was prepared to cut out whatever Jesus didn't like. That's a good, simple definition of repentance.

Many people I know have been baptised without even being asked to produce that much proof of repentance. I baptise people not on profession of faith but on proof of repentance. Paul said, "I was not disobedient to the heavenly vision, so I...". Could you write down the completion of the sentence? I have never met a Christian who could tell me. He said, "so I preached repentance to the Gentiles that they should turn to God and prove their repentance by their deeds". That I have never heard preached: prove their repentance by their deeds, not by their works. You can find it in Acts 26. No, I actually don't give chapter and verse numbers ever. They are not inspired by the Lord. I just say, "Look up the book of Acts." I want people to search the scriptures, not to look them up.

So, repentance is something that we need to *do*. Fruits worthy of repentance produce proof — repentance by our deeds. Faith, therefore, is not something that we think, or say, or feel, but it's something that we do. When our three children were little, we had a game called "Faith" to teach them what faith was. We would go to the stairs in the middle of the house, and they would climb up about five stairs. I would stand at the bottom, with my hands behind my back and they would say, "Daddy, if we jump, will you catch us?" I would say, "I might. I'm not promising." They would stand there, swaying with anticipation in their little tummies, contemplating whether they should throw themselves out. I think it was their equivalent of video nasties in those days. Then one of them would jump and I would catch them. That gave confidence to the other two and they would jump and I would catch them.

They loved this game called "Faith". What I was trying to teach them was: "You don't have faith in me until you jump. I don't know if you trust me until you do something about it." That is exactly how James, in chapter two of his letter, describes faith. Consider the faith of Rahab, the prostitute, the faith of Abraham; in Hebrews 11, the chapter of heroes of faith, in every case they *did* faith. Noah believed and he built an ark. Faith was something they did, a risk taken. They would have fallen flat on their faces if it didn't work.

There was a joke going around the churches in England about a man walking across a field on a dark, foggy night. He fell over the cliff at the edge of the field, and he was falling down this deep valley when he managed to get hold of a tree growing out of the cliff. He grabbed it with both hands and he was hanging there in the dark and the fog, wondering how far it was to the bottom. He called up and said, "Is there anybody up there?"

A deep voice in the clouds said, "Yes, my son, I am here."

"Can you get me out of this?"

"Yes."

"What do I have to do?"

"Let go of the tree."

"Is there anybody else up there?"

This is faith. It's taking a risk. It is doing something to show that you trust. I was preaching in a large church in Germany, a brand new beautiful building in the centre of a large city. I happened to say, "How many of you in the congregation believe in me?" There was a long silence and then about five hands went up, including a very well-dressed lady in the front row. Then I said, "How many of you believe that I exist?" Every hand went up. See, if you word the appeal correctly you get a bigger response! But I said, "You all believe that I exist, but only five have said you believe in me. Even those five, I don't know if they believe in me. They've professed faith in me, but I don't know if they do."

I pointed to the well-dressed lady in the front row. Never preach to an individual in a congregation, you will come unstuck! I said to her, "You put your hand up; you believe in me." I said, "I don't know if you do. You've said you do." But I continued, "Would you give me all your money to look after? If you do that, I would know that you believed in me. You would have proved it by your deed; I would then know that you trust me." The whole place went deadly quiet. Nobody smiled and, you know, you could feel the ice forming.

Afterwards I said to the pastor, "Why did everybody freeze when I said that?"

"She's the richest lady in this city. Her husband owned all the property in the centre of the city, and he has died and left it to her." I gathered she'd given all the money for the new church building. So, I am afraid that particular piece of homiletics came to a dismal failure.

But the point I was making was absolutely right. The Lord is saying to us, "How do I know you believe in me?" You say you do, but you don't believe in the Lord until you take a risk, until you do something that will be a disaster if he is not there. Think about it. That is why Rahab, the harlot, the prostitute in Jericho, pinned her future to the people of Israel and the God of Israel. The risk she was taking! Had the people of Jericho found out her real attitude, she would have been a dead woman.

Consider Abraham offering Isaac. What a risk to take. We know that he had faith because he believed that God would raise Isaac from the dead, and there had never been a resurrection of the dead before that. But that is what he believed. He took the risk of being prepared to kill his son because he believed that God would raise him from the dead. We are told that in scripture. We know it because when he left his servants at the foot of the mountain and said, "My son and I are going up the mountain," he said, "we're going up to worship the Lord and we will come back to you".

James says Rahab and Abraham proved their faith by their deeds. It was an *active* faith. They actually did something that proved they trusted the Lord. So, this very active view of repentance and faith has tended to be replaced by an inward, mental repentance and faith that may even get as far as word, but doesn't get as far as deed. If there is one thing I feel that evangelists are failing to do, it is helping inquirers to repent, *really* repent — put things right, and this is my second point.

I was preaching at an evangelistic crusade for three days in Aberdeen. That is where all the oil comes ashore from the North Sea. I used to take an evangelistic crusade about once a year to prove that I'm not an evangelist! It is good. The Lord still embarrasses me, but nevertheless, I am not an evangelist. I have found the secret of happily serving the Lord is to live within your gifting and not try and be what he has not gifted you to be or called you to be. But I still take occasional evangelistic crusades. People still get converted; no one is more surprised than I am.

On the second night in the theatre in Aberdeen, a girl came up to me. She was crying, her face was all blotchy red. She was shaking; she was obviously deeply disturbed. She said, "Mr. Pawson, you frustrate me."

I asked, "Why? How?"

She said, "You've made me want to be a Christian."

I replied, "But that's why I came. That's why I'm here. What's wrong with that?"

"I have tried to be a Christian for eighteen months. I have gone forward at every appeal, at every evangelistic meeting, including the visit of Luis Palau, the South American evangelist. I've been counselled. I've been to classes. I've done everything they've told me, but nothing has changed. Nothing has happened. I gave it up. A few weeks ago, I said, 'There's nothing in this Christianity.' But a friend of mine has dragged me to the meeting tonight and you have stirred it all up all over again. You've made me want to be a Christian. I have tried. I've done everything they've told me."

I asked the Lord for a word of knowledge, then looked her in the eye and asked, "Who are you living with?"

"A young man," she answered.

I said, "Are you married to him?"

"No."

"Are you living as if you were married?"

"Yes."

"Why aren't you married?"

"Well he doesn't believe in marriage. He said it's just a piece of paper; the important thing is that we love each other."

I said, "Well, if he leaves you tomorrow, he's not breaking any promises because he never made any."

She replied, "He won't leave me; he loves me too much."

I then said, "Well you've got a very difficult decision to make. I wish I could make it for you, but I can't. You've got to decide which man you want to live with: Jesus or the young man, but you can't live with both. Jesus won't join in an arrangement like that."

Then she got really angry, saying, "No one else told me to do that."

I said, "But I'm trying to help you."

I would love to say that she made the right decision and was gloriously saved. I can't tell you that. She ran out of the building, sobbing her eyes out.

Straight away as she went, I understand how the Lord felt when the rich young ruler went away. Jesus was saying to the rich young ruler: it is your money or me. For that man it was a choice that he couldn't make, and he went away sad. But I felt the feelings of Jesus. You know, you can be so anxious to get someone converted that you lower the standards of repentance. That girl had not been told to repent. She had been told how to receive Jesus into her life. She had been given all the right words, the sinner's prayer, the lot, but she had never been taught how to repent.

Of repentance and faith, I would say that the most neglected in modern evangelism is repentance. We assume that it can come later. Indeed, I have heard people advocating,

"Get them to faith first and then they can repent." That was never the order in the New Testament. It was always: repent and believe. You repent, not towards Jesus. You *repent toward God* and then you *believe in* Jesus. Because it is God whose laws you have broken. It is God whose anger you have aroused. It is God whose love you have spurned. It is God's judgment you have deserved. I don't believe in telling people about Jesus until they realise they need to get right with God. Then Jesus makes such sense — that he came to get over the problem.

So, I find that Luther's understanding of faith and repentance was too passive. He was so frightened of people thinking that they could earn or merit salvation that he cut out any thought of actions of our own. But works of repentance and works of faith are what Paul meant when he told people to *obey the gospel*. That is a remarkable statement. In 2 Thessalonians 1 he talks about people being judged for not obeying the gospel. Not for not accepting it, for not believing it—for not *obeying* it.

This whole emphasis of the New Testament on *doing* faith, on *doing* repentance, is not to merit or earn in any way. But it is the way to appropriate the salvation that is ours. So, you get this apparent contradiction between Paul and James, which when you look at it more carefully is not a contradiction at all but two aspects of the same thing that need to be held together and make action an important part.

Now we move to the third thing. Luther, focusing on justification by faith, left two impressions, which need revising. The first was the impression that we are saved in a moment. We are *justified* in a moment, but salvation is a process. It doesn't happen in a moment. But the emphasis was: "You are justified in a moment and heaven is yours in a moment. You now have eternal security in Christ." To say that is to leave the impression that you are saved in a moment. The result is that, invariably today, evangelicals use the word "saved" in the past tense. "I was saved twenty years ago," someone tells me or, "We had seven people saved last Sunday night in church." I always correct them and I always say, "You *began* to be saved twenty years ago. You had seven people who *began* to be saved last Sunday night," because salvation is not in a moment; justification is, salvation is not. It is a process that can take a lifetime and more. As I have told you, I am not saved yet but I am on the way.

What scholars know perfectly well, preachers should tell their congregations: that the verb "save" in the New Testament is in three tenses: past, present and future. We have been saved; we are being saved; we will be saved. Of those three tenses, the most are future: we will be. The whole emphasis in the New Testament is that we are looking forward to being saved. Let us take one or two random texts.

Take one from Romans first. Paul says, "We are nearer our salvation than when we first believed." Now what does that mean? The impression has been given by so many preachers, "Oh, but I was saved when I first responded. I'm saved. I was saved then." But no, they began to be. Unfortunately, we have given the impression that "saved" means "saved from hell". The gospel becomes a kind of fire insurance policy. But Jesus did not come to save us from hell. That is a bonus thrown in. He is called Jesus because he came to save us from our sins—all of them. It is in the plural there.

In other words, salvation is to make us perfect, sinless, with no trace of the Fall in us, to restore the image of God in each of us perfectly. That is salvation. Now my wife has tremendous faith. She is very solid on most things, but there is one thing I teach that she has real problems believing. It is when I tell her that one day her husband will be perfect. She says, "If I based my faith on experience, I couldn't believe it, but I'll try and base my faith on the Word of God, and that he who began a good work in me will complete it." But I have got to believe that one day my wife will be perfect. I do remind her of that, though I think the Lord has a bigger job with me than with her.

Nevertheless, to be made perfect is to be saved. That is New Testament thinking. It begins with justification, when God treats us as if we were righteous, when righteousness is *imputed* to us. But that is only the beginning. The next task, which takes a lot of time, is *imparting* his righteousness to us, making us righteous, not just in title but in reality. That can take a lifetime of faith. We will only be completed, I believe, when Jesus returns and we see him as he is. Then we shall be like him. That is salvation.

Now the other impression that has been left by defining salvation in terms of justification is the "once saved, always saved" impression. Now here I may be walking into the porridge, nevertheless I will. I believe that that cliché, which is not in the Bible, "once saved, always saved", has done more damage to the Christian pursuit of holiness than anything else. People are resting on a past decision, a past experience, rather than pressing on toward the mark because they have heard "once saved, always saved".

You see, in my definition of "saved" I am not "once saved" yet. In the day when the image of God is permanently restored in me I am going to shout loudly so that all of heaven can hear, "Once saved, always saved," because then it will be true because I will be once saved. You see, what it is saying is, "Once justified", not once saved. These two impressions, salvation is a moment and that once you've got it you can't lose it, I believe are doing tremendous damage.

Christians living in open adultery come to me and tell me, "It's alright; I'm still going to heaven. I'm still saved; I don't want you to worry about me." I tell them, "Do you realise you're risking the whole future? You're saying that

God would condemn an unbeliever for doing what you, a believer, are doing, but he won't condemn you?" God has no favourites. His judgment is absolutely fair. We must all appear before the judgment seat of Christ to receive the things done in the body. But the "once saved, always saved" idea has really gripped people. Once you are justified, here is your ticket to heaven. Everything is absolutely secure for the future.

I think we have got to look at that very carefully. I have written a book called, *Once Saved, Always Saved?* — note the question mark. In it, I have referred to eighty passages in the New Testament, warning us not to lose our salvation. They are saying salvation is a process, a process which can be interrupted and even fail to be completed. That is my understanding of scripture. If you have a different opinion of scripture to that, I ask you to look really carefully into the New Testament. Those eighty passages cover every author in the New Testament, and each is saying: Don't lose what you've got.

If I just take a random selection of those eighty, Jesus in John's Gospel says, "I am the true vine; stay in me. Abide in me; reside in me." The simplest part is "stay in me" — because I don't have eternal life in me. I do have it in Christ. Eternal life is not in the branches, it is in the vine. If I stay in the vine I go on having eternal life. What if I step out of the vine? Jesus said that branches that don't stay in the vine wither. They are fruitless and they are cut off and burned. There is a relationship with the vine that means "continued everlasting life". But it is *in him*, not me. As John says, this life is in the Son. Whoever is in the Son is having life and whoever is not is not having life.

If we translate John 3:16 correctly it says this: "For so God once loved the world that he once gave his only son that whoever goes on believing in him will not once perish, but go on having eternal life." Does that alter the feel of the verse for you? I am translating the Greek. The first two verbs are in the aorist tense, which referred to one event: when he once loved the world, when he once gave his Son. But the other two verbs are in the present continuous tense, which is: whoever goes on believing in me will go on having eternal life.

John wrote his Gospel to Christians. The fourth Gospel is not one to give to the unbeliever. It is written to mature Christians who have known the Lord for years, to keep them believing that Jesus is divine, because in Ephesus, where it was written, there were people like Cerinthus teaching a Jesus more like the Jesus of the Jehovah's Witnesses. So, John says, "If everything Jesus said and did was in books, the world couldn't contain the books. But these are written so that you may go on believing that Jesus is the Son of God, and going on believing you may go on having eternal life." That opens up the whole Gospel in a totally new way — even John 3:16 changes.

So, these two wrong impressions – on the one hand, that when you believed in Christ the first time, your salvation was complete, and the other impression, that therefore it cannot be taken from you now – I believe have to be re-examined in the light of scripture, and corrected.

Next, the *comparative* (and I italicise that word) neglect of sanctification by faith. There has been so much emphasis on justification by faith, that there was a comparative neglect of sanctification by faith – in a word: holiness. John Wesley is one of my heroes, because one of his first colleagues was a man called John Pawson, one of my ancestors. He said, "Methodism has been raised up to spread scriptural holiness throughout this land." There are historians who claim (though I'm not supporting their claim) that John Wesley saved England from the French Revolution because he spread holiness. He was the great preacher of sanctification by faith, not sanctification by works. For as Paul says, "The gospel is faith from beginning to end". That is sanctification by faith.

Now I find that preachers today fall into two traps when it comes to holiness. On the one hand, preachers imply that holiness is not essential to go to heaven. It is almost taught in terms of: it is an optional extra for which there will be a bonus reward in heaven, but it is no longer considered essential or even part of the basic gospel. But in my New Testament, sanctification by faith is just as important, if not more important than justification by faith. For without holiness no one will see the Lord. In other words, we are to offer a gospel of sanctification.

Now I am not just talking theology or theory, because I preach in top security prisons and in gypsy camps in Britain. Here you are dealing with people who are notorious for bad deeds. In the top security prison I go to I am preaching to murderers and drug dealers, all of whom are in for life. I never get a better audience. I can preach for three hours to them and they want more, they are just so hungry. But what I offer them is a gospel of righteousness from God, a gospel, quite simply, of being good people. I offer sanctification as well as justification as the gospel.

It is not a question of "you can be forgiven, but you must be holy". That is not the gospel. Nor is it "you can be forgiven and needn't be holy". Both of those are travesties of the gospel. My gospel is: *you can be forgiven and you can be holy*. When I tell these men that they can be saints, not just in title but in deed, that they can be such people that one day they will sit with Christ on the throne and judge other people — you should see their eyes. And the same goes for when I tell people in prison for life that one day they will be the judge! I say, "Then you will have to be very just," because most of them feel unjustly treated by human judges.

To me, the gospel is not just your sins can be forgiven, but you can be made a saint. You can become the person you long to be in your best moments, not just one moment before you die. A life of faith can make you like Jesus. Well, I believe that comparative neglect of imparted righteousness as well as imputed righteousness, to use the theological terms, is only half a gospel. We are offering righteousness to people, not just forgiveness. We are offering holiness. We had better live up to our gospel if we do, and show signs of being made better men and women ourselves.

These are some of the notes that we need to be sounding today to complete Luther's Reformation of the gospel.

CHURCH AND STATE

I have told you that I am a reformation rather than a revival man. I believe that the Lord is calling the Church to put things right so that then he may bless us. The order is reformation first, revival second, as far as I understand the Lord's will. Why should he revive a Church that is being openly disobedient to his Word? I don't understand why we expect him to do that.

We have seen that when Luther majored on justification by faith, all the four things I mentioned in the last chapter followed, because if you over-emphasise one doctrine the others get out of balance. The fifth effect was that he focused on the second person of the Trinity almost exclusively. I remember the classic conversation he had with Johann von Staupitz, his mentor in the monastery. When von Staupitz said, "Martin, if you sweep away relics, prayers to saints ... What will you put in their place?" Luther's classic answer was, "Jesus Christ; man only needs Jesus Christ."

That was the focus of his theology. Therefore (comparatively), he neglected the third person of the Trinity. It was left to the twentieth century to rediscover the Holy Spirit in practice. It was on the very first day of the twentieth century, in Topeka, Kansas, that the students of a Bible college were determined to experience Acts 2 for themselves. This was a revolutionary idea: that Pentecost was not just a historical event, marking the birth of the Church, but an existential event to be repeated in the lives of individual Christians.

I have searched in vain for any mention in Luther of the gifts of the Spirit, or even the fruit of the Spirit, and there is certainly no mention of the baptism in the Holy Spirit. So that whole dimension came to life in the twentieth century. It was not new. If you study Church history carefully you find that there were charismatic outbreaks, or renewals, right through Church history.

For example, one of the great patron saints in my country is Saint David of Wales. You may have heard of him. But Saint David was appointed, or chosen, to be a bishop. For his ordination he wanted to go to Jerusalem because he felt that if he was made a bishop there he would have a special anointing. In those days pilgrimage was quite a large part of Christian piety, and especially pilgrimage to the Holy Land. There were no jumbo jets in those days, so he set off with two monks to walk to Jerusalem. I have a copy of the diary kept by those two monks. This is one of the entries: "Ye Holy Father David came to Lyon in Gaul. And there ye Holy Father David was baptised in ye Holy Ghost and spake in other tongues as in the days of ye apostles."

I love to tell the Welsh about this because they are stuck in 1904 and we are going back now to the fifth century, when David spoke in tongues and was "baptised in ye Holy Ghost". So, it was not a new thing, but it was a major rediscovery of it. The Pentecostal stream of the Christian Church is now the fastest growing and is about to become the largest stream in Christendom for the twenty-first century. All that happened in the last hundred years or so.

Luther, of course, never saw all this and didn't talk about it, and didn't expect Christians to have their own personal

Pentecost or a baptism in the Spirit, even though all our four Gospels begin with a promise that Jesus would baptise in the Holy Ghost. It is such a fundamental thing. John the Baptist said two things about Jesus. One: he is the Lamb of God who takes away the sins of the world. Two: he will baptise in the Holy Spirit. These two must go together because a life that has been emptied of sin, from which sin has been taken away, is in a very dangerous situation, said Jesus, unless it is filled up with something else. There is nothing so dangerous as a Christian emptied of sin. There is a vacuum there that will drag more demons back in, says Jesus. So, these two things must go together.

But it is interesting, the Church historically has picked up one of these two things, but not the other. The world over, the quotation "the Lamb of God that takes away the sin of the world" is used in liturgy, but the baptising in the Holy Spirit has been left out of all the historic liturgies of the Church. When you study the Bible carefully, John the Baptist only said "the Lamb of God that takes away the sin of the world" once, and privately to two disciples, whereas his statement "He will baptise in the Holy Spirit" was made frequently and publicly. Indeed, the Greek suggests that every time he preached he announced that the baptiser in the Holy Spirit would follow him. So, isn't it strange that the Church has taken up the one private remark to two people and blown it up into all the liturgies of the world and has ignored the public, repeated announcement that Jesus would be the baptiser?

John the Baptist was, of course, very aware that his baptism was limited. It could only deal with people's past. It could only clean up their past. It couldn't do anything for their future. To this day, water baptism's main effect is on your past and doesn't help you for your future. For that, you need another baptism – in the Holy Spirit. It is the third person who brings sanctification by faith. Again, we see that an over-emphasis on justification by faith, which neglected sanctification by faith, therefore put all the emphasis on Jesus and his work, and did not put the emphasis on the Holy Spirit's work. Jesus did everything needed for our justification, but it is the Holy Spirit who works our sanctification in us, by giving us both purity and power. So here we have the fifth thing that is neglected today.

One of the things that has become characteristic of contemporary evangelism is the appeal to *receive Jesus*. Often it is reported that, "We had so many people who received Christ." This is not a biblical term. From the day of Pentecost onwards, the verb "receive" was transferred from the second to the third person of the Trinity, exclusively. While Jesus was on earth people could receive him or not. Literally, they could receive him into their homes.

John 1:12 is a historical statement in the past tense, yet it is used in every booklet I have bought on how to become a Christian. The literal translation is "to as many as *received* him", not, "to as many as *receive* him". "To them he gave" not power but "authority [*exousia*] to become the sons of God, even those who believed in his name". This does not say, as most preachers quote it: as many as receive him. In context, it is past tense: "He came to his own place and his own people did not receive him. But as many as received him, to them he gave authority to become sons of God." It is not a text to be used in evangelism now, because while he was here you could receive him, you could ask him into your home. But after he ascended to heaven, and is now at the right hand of the Father, you cannot receive him. You can receive his deputy on earth, who has taken his place, the Holy Spirit.

It is not just a matter of wording. A profound difference has taken place in evangelism by talking of the second person as if he is the third. To put it quite simply: if we are counselling an enquirer we need to help them to: repent toward God, believe in Jesus, and receive the Holy Spirit. You check me out in scripture. The apostles, preaching the gospel, never told people to receive Jesus or, even worse, to invite him into their lives or invite him into their hearts. None of this kind of language is in the New Testament. It all comes from nineteenth-century American revivalism. Our evangelism has been so deeply influenced from across the Atlantic that I am afraid we have all fallen into it and urged people to receive Jesus and invite him into their lives or commit themselves to Jesus. Why don't we go back to the New Testament and say, "Repent toward God, believe in the Lord Jesus, and receive the Holy Spirit"? In other words, evangelism, to accord with New Testament teaching, should establish a Trinitarian relationship with the enquirer from the beginning.

Someone may say: "Yes, I agree with your point, but what about Revelation 3: 'Behold I stand at the door and knock?'"

What about that? It has nothing to do with evangelism.

"No, but receiving Jesus."

It has nothing to do with it; that is addressed to a church. It is a prophetic promise that if Jesus has left your church, one member can get him back in. It is addressed to believers; it is addressed to a church.

When I wrote my first book, *The Normal Christian Birth*, it grew out of a burden that everywhere I went, Christians had been badly birthed. An evangelist is a midwife. It is very important how people come to Christ, not only for their own sake, but because the way they came will be perpetuated in the way they tell other people to come. That is the problem. Billy Graham, for example, never mentions baptism, yet he was baptised three times. He can write a whole book about being born again and never mention baptism, which is astonishing when you think of it. But baptism played no part whatever in his conversion. So, the way he came is the way he leads others.

I have found that with evangelists – they invariably try to bring others into the kingdom the way they came in. We are all guilty of this. I found that many Christians had problems because they missed out on a vital element in their birth and therefore were sickly Christians or weak Christians because they hadn't had a good start. I even went to our local midwife and said, "Would you write down what we need to do for a baby when it is born." I was astonished; I thought you just pulled them out. But she wrote four foolscap sheets of directions as to how to birth a baby. There was a corresponding element in being born again, similar to what she told me.

But in my book, my thesis is that if you are going to bring someone into the kingdom you need to do four things for them: help them to repent toward God, believe in the Lord Jesus, receive the Holy Spirit, and be baptised in the name of the Father, Son and Holy Spirit. Only if we have done all four have we properly birthed a Christian. I meet so many Christians with problems. They come to me and say, "Can you help me with this problem?" I say, "Before we talk about your problem, tell me how you were born again. Just tell me about your conversion." I listen to see if all these four things were present. Invariably, there have been one, two, or even three that have never been brought into their birth.

The particular one that I am most troubled by is that there has been little or no repentance. A thirty-second sinner's prayer is not repentance. It really isn't. There have been no deeds of repentance in that. So, you can read my theory of the normal Christian birth. It has now been called a classic and is being used as a textbook in many Bible colleges. Thank God for that. Consider Hebrews chapter 6. It is all there.

When I wrote my book, I bought thirty-six booklets by

well-known evangelistic organisations on how to become a Christian. There were two texts in every one of those booklets: John 1:12 and Revelation 3:20, both of them irrelevant to helping an enquirer to get into the kingdom.

I speak emotionally about this, but I have met so many Christians with problems and all they have done is believe in Jesus. Then I say, "Well let's get you properly birthed and let's fill in the gap." When we do that, either the problem gets much smaller or it even disappears altogether. The problem goes right back to their birth as a Christian, that they were not properly handled and not well birthed. Well there it is, but that book is probably the most important one I have written. As I say, evangelists are now using it. I get letter after letter from pastors and evangelists, "We're getting so much better-quality conversions. People are really becoming strong, healthy babies and growing and maturing more quickly."

Let us take another text that we really should use. When Peter preached the first evangelistic sermon on the day of Pentecost, the people said, "What must we do?" The key word there is "do". They were told what they should do: "Repent and be baptised, each one of you, for the forgiveness of sins, and you will receive the gift of the Holy Spirit." That is a pretty complete enquirer counselling text, but I have never seen it used in modern evangelism. Isn't that amazing? I call it the "Peter package". Many people are now using the Peter package to counsel an enquirer: repent, believe, be baptised, and receive the gift of the Spirit. Notice where receive is related to the third person. That is surely the technique that should govern all our evangelism, yet it is carefully ignored by most evangelists today. But it was Peter's answer.

So far we have been talking about the gospel, what we preach, the message, and how we preach salvation and how we apply it when we preach. But now we move on to much more controversial ground. This is where I "walk straight into the porridge" again. We are going to think now about the church we *practise*.

We are thinking now not just of the individual side of reformation and salvation, but about the corporate side of reformation, which is urgently needed in the twenty-first century. We want to have a Church that is going to last. What I am going to describe for you is what I believe is God's answer to the kind of church that will stay the course in the twenty-first century. It is a very different century. We are in an entirely different context even to the twentieth century right now. I'll explain that as we go along.

I finished the previous five reformations with a look at the rediscovery of the Holy Spirit in the twentieth century, which has inevitably affected our understanding of church life. That rediscovery has led to changes to church life which have affected almost every church. An initial, superficial observation: the number of churches that now have a little band of musicians or orchestras, backing singers and microphones. It is amazing how even the oldest, most staid churches have adopted this kind of worship.

We live in a global village now and communication means that a new chorus, written in New Zealand, is sung around the world within three months. It is quite astonishing how we copy each other the world over. This happens with any new trend. As soon as people started waving banners in worship it suddenly went around the world in months – everywhere. As soon as we had microphones and amplifiers, my life became dangerous! On most of the platforms that I speak on, I feel I'm standing in the middle of a telephone exchange, with wires everywhere and my feet are tangled up! All that is new, and technology is spreading things so quickly now.

I plunge in with the first big reformation issue. I believe

the day of the State Church is over and that State Churches will not survive to the end of the twenty-first century. I will now expand on that with a brief historical survey. In the Old Testament, religion and State were one and the same thing in Israel, which is what we call a "theocracy", where the rules were made not by a government but by God himself. God ruled Israel. They could rebel against his rule, but his was the only rule they saw.

Therefore, the laws of Moses are a complete mixture of ceremonial, liturgical, criminal, and domestic laws. You can't distinguish really. They are so mixed up in the Law of Moses. You are dealing with crime one minute, then with family life, then with the government of Israel and the kings of Israel. It is completely interlocked. You may try and separate it out, but you will destroy the Word of God if you do, because it was totally interlinked – under the same rule.

That meant that it was legitimate for them to fight, physically, for the establishment and the defence of Israel. But when you turn to the New Testament there is a radical separation of Church and State. You render to Caesar what is Caesar's and to God what is God's. There are two distinct loyalties. Of course, Martin Luther made a great deal of this double morality: the duty of the Christian to the State in which they are and to the Church of which they are part.

So, in the New Testament the kingdom of God is not of this world – meaning not *out of* this world, but not *from* this world – and therefore the servants of Jesus are not commissioned to fight for it. For example, "Else my servants would fight," said Jesus, "if my kingdom was of this world". For three hundred years, Church and State were totally separate. Of course, it meant persecution because Christianity was for a long time a *religio illicita* to the Roman Empire whereas Judaism had been accepted.

The Roman Empire was syncretistic. When they

conquered a new people they took the god of that people and put that god alongside all the others in the big building in Rome called the Pantheon, which you can still see today. The Jews, of course, refused to do that. They said, "No, we worship the one and only God." Amazingly, they were given official recognition. They were called "atheists" because they wouldn't believe in the Roman Pantheon of gods, but they were a *religio licita* – a legal religion with full permission to practise.

At first the early Christians were seen as part of Judaism, as a Jewish sect, and therefore were under the umbrella of following a legal religion. But as the Gentiles became Christian and as the Church clearly became a different religious body to Judaism, then the question arose: would the empire recognise Christianity? The answer was no. Of course, it meant death, martyrdom for many early Christians. Once a year, on a day called "The Lord's Day", or literally "The Lordly Day", every Roman citizen had to stand before a bust of Caesar, raise his right arm, throw incense on the altar and say, "Caesar is lord" – three little words. Christians refused to say that and paid for it with their lives in horrible deaths.

That is the reference in Revelation chapter one: "I was in the Spirit on the Lord's Day". That is not Sunday. If you look at the phrase, it was the Lordly Day, the day on which they all had to say, "Caesar is lord". The whole of Revelation is really a manual for martyrdom, to prepare the churches for this crisis of refusing to say "Caesar is lord", and practising a *religio illicita*. That continued with more or less furious bouts of persecution for three hundred years.

The Church never grew so quickly as in those three hundred years. Today the Church under pressure grows in quantity and quality. When the Church is not under pressure it declines. I could illustrate that from around the world.

For a Church that is persecuted, the blood of the martyrs is the seed of the Church. That is still true. In one recent year, there were some 264,000 estimated martyrs for Jesus. This is not the case in parts of the world where we have general social and political acceptance, though where we decline in numbers. I envy those under persecution.

I remember going to Czechoslovakia when it was still behind the Iron Curtain. I told the people in the Church there, "We pray for you." They were absolutely astonished. They came to me afterwards and said, "You're praying for us? We're praying for you. You're in far greater need than we are." Sure enough, their churches were packed, even though it cost them to be there. I was coming home to empty churches in England. I realised how patronising I had been to say, "We pray for you."

I was with 120 pastors in East Germany and they told me, "Bring back Honecker." I said, "But Honecker was a communist dictator." They replied, "Yes, but the churches were much better in those days. Now all that our members want is a tenth-hand Mercedes car. Back then they wanted to pray." These 120 pastors were bemoaning the Berlin Wall coming down and communism going. It just shook me to think like that. I thought in my naivety they would be welcoming the freedom. But no, they were now overcome by the materialism and consumerism of the West. The spiritual quality of their churches had gone right down. As pastors, they were so concerned.

Let us go back to the subject. Was it the best thing that happened to the Church, or the worst thing, that the Roman Emperor was converted? It is a very debatable point. For the first time, Christians had political and even military power. Christianity could now be imposed by the State and sanctioned as the official religion. Therefore, the whole situation changed from the top down. Church and State began to be related again. That continued for the next thousand years.

It is interesting that, about a century later, St Augustine wrote *The City of God*. If you read that carefully, he is dealing with the collapse of the Roman Empire, but saying that out of the collapse will come a new State Church/Church State. Augustine was the first major theologian of the Church to justify the use of force by Christians. He outlined the Just War Theory. He also picked on one word in one of our Lord's parables, where the Lord said, "Go out into the highways and byways and compel them to come in." He took that word "compel" and built a huge theology on it: that force or persuasion was justified if the end was spiritual. That of course led, inevitably, to things like the Inquisition and the Crusades, and the Christian use of political and military force. That was a huge change. Up to Constantine, Christians had never had any worldly force to use. They had had to rely on the power of the Holy Spirit alone. So began a thousand years of struggle between Holy Roman emperors and popes as to who was the top dog.

I am simplifying grossly the history of the Middle Ages, but there is a tension there between Church and State because they are now so closely related that one is wanting to control the other. Sometimes it was the Holy Roman emperor who was on top and sometimes it was the Pope. But that is the situation into which Martin Luther was born. It had been a situation for a thousand years, where the State made religious decisions for the citizens. When the rulers of the State made a decision, the citizens had to follow. That was the power that Luther mainly used to bring Protestantism to northern Europe. Change the rulers, and their State would have to change also. They changed the Elector of Saxony, and Saxony was now a Protestant state. In other words, reform came from the top. The power that was used to spread the

Reformation was the power of the State.

We call the Reformers in the Reformation "magisterial" – those who used the power of the State to bring about reformation. But once again, the tension was: which was on top—the State or the Church? You had Luther's situation, where the State was over the church, and you had Calvin's situation in Geneva, where the Church was over the State. But they both had inherited – and neither of them did anything really about it – a State-Church interlock, and still kept the concept of a State Church.

So around the year 1000, for example, a lot of States in Europe changed from paganism to Christianity and the Catholic variety or a Celtic variety from Ireland. Later, at the time of the Reformation, one state after another in northern Europe became Protestant, not because the people changed or because the Holy Spirit was bringing about this change, but because the state now adopted this new Protestant religion. They were far more successful in this in northern Europe than in southern, which remained staunchly Catholic. In between different cantons in Switzerland, the north became Protestant and the south stayed Catholic. You have that division to this very day, and of course they used to fight each other.

Zwingli, the third most famous Reformer, died in battle. I have stood at his memorial in the middle of the battlefield in Switzerland and remembered that he went to arms to defend Protestantism against a Catholic army, and perished in so doing. Still to this day, you have Swiss Guards in the Vatican, looking after the Pope, wearing the uniforms of the Middle Ages. It is a very mixed-up situation.

So, we have from Luther the idea of a State-led church. This spread to England. It spread to Norway, Sweden, Denmark and Germany. In my country there is an anomaly because Scotland followed Geneva and Calvin. So there the

Church was considered above the State, but in England it was the reverse and led, of course, to Henry VIII's break with the Pope and making himself head of our Church of England. That is how the Church of England came to be. Of course, after Henry VIII you had four changes, from Catholic to Protestant, to Catholic, to Protestant, and terrible persecution as each tried to impose their religion on the State. So, Mary would try to impose Roman Catholicism, only to be followed by Elizabeth, who tried to impose a mixture of Lutheranism and Anglicanism. That is what we have inherited.

But I want to tell you with all the emphasis I can, the day of the State Church is over. "Christendom" is a dead concept. That was the name coined to combine Christianity and the kingdom of this world. The word "Christendom" is a combination of "Christianity" and "kingdom". That has gone. The trouble is we have all been brought up in a situation where we have had support, even financial support, from the State, and where we have had the sanction of the State that is all changing rapidly. The reason is that in democratic countries governments are increasingly non-Christian, and today even anti-Christian, particularly where it is a left-wing government. That is bringing terrific pressure on the Church in terms of doctrine and ethics to make clear decisions for the future.

So, we cannot any longer rely on State support or sanction for the preservation of the Church. We must prepare now for the day when that is over. It is already beginning to head that way in Sweden, and in Germany, and it will come to Norway. What we need to do is prepare our people. How do we do that? Well, the Three-Self Church in China is a model. It is self-governing, self-propagating and self-supporting. We are going to have to teach our people that they will need to pay for everything the Church is and does. We will need to develop New Testament giving. Not tithing – that is Old

Testament – but giving, which is often far more generous and unselfish.

We need to prepare our people for persecution. With this whole development, we are now increasingly in the hands of godless States and godless politicians, for whom relativism is their religion, multiculturalism, and the manifesto. Thus, we are into a totally new situation, where State-Church links are out of date. Therefore, we have got to adapt our churches now or they won't survive when that support is withdrawn. That is what I am telling people in our country—where some Anglican clergy are paid out of investments. But we do have "Gift Aid". If I give a gift to a church, the government will give the tax I paid on that amount back. That is one way we receive support from the State. I am telling churches, "If you have a lot of tax refunds through that scheme, don't put the money into your current account. Use it only for capital expenditure so that your people can learn to support a current account from their giving." Then when that tax refund is withdrawn, as it most certainly will be, all the privileges we have enjoyed through State religion are going to be withdrawn in this century. I am absolutely sure of that.

I believe that Church history is coming full circle, and we are going to be back in the Roman Empire period for all practical purposes. The Church will be a persecuted minority, and I am happy about that; it will grow. But we (particularly some younger people) are going to have to adapt to being in the same situation as the Church was for the first hundred years before it managed to get hold of political authority. Well, that is my prediction. You can weigh and judge that before the Lord. Please don't believe anything I say, unless he confirms it for you. We will therefore have to rely purely on the Holy Spirit's power and on the generosity and support of God's people. But I am preparing people for persecution.

Ten years ago, when I first began to say to the churches of

Britain, "Are you preparing your members for persecution?" they laughed. They thought this was ridiculous, because I have been brought up in a country that was supposed to be a Christian country, but where Christianity at least was respected, part of the national ethos and very privileged. I didn't think I would live to see preachers of the gospel put in prison in England. But that happened quite recently. Of course, with the increasing takeover of our country by Islam we are being pressured by Sharia law. The major persecution is coming from Islam, and is already happening.

A friend of mine put a poster outside his church, "Jesus is the only way to God." He was immediately persecuted because of the Islamic pressure in that community. He was prosecuted for "disturbing the peace" for putting that poster up. The anti-Christian legislation now is really extraordinary; we are losing freedom of speech in England. I am in legal difficulties because of some of the books I have written. My publishers have to consult lawyers to defend some of my books. The only element that was deemed to be controversial in one of them was that homosexual practice is wrong in God's sight. But a Bill was introduced to Parliament which would have meant that if anybody were to take offence at what you say, then that might have led to a criminal prosecution. Freedom of speech is on the way out in my country, very rapidly, and this means freedom to preach the gospel and freedom to preach Christian moral standards. So, I am afraid I am expecting legal trouble, and I am ready for it. I don't mind going to court myself, but I don't want other people to have to because of me. It really becomes a bit difficult.

So, we are going right back to the days when Christianity was a *religio illicita*. In the face of relativism, syncretism and multiculturalism we are now the minority that doesn't fit. Our people are just not ready for this. Do you know that an investigation agency in London has been asked to compile a confidential dossier on the private lives of all major Christian leaders and preachers so that they can be publicly humiliated? That gives you the main approach for preparing people for persecution. It is very simple: be sure that you are living a holy life and that you cannot be blamed by the authorities, that you cannot be exposed and weakened because they have knowledge about you. Prepare your people by urging them to live righteous lives. To be blamed for righteousness is an honour and a privilege for a Christian; to be blamed for unrighteousness is a shame. Read 1 Peter carefully.

That is the first great reformation of the Church: I believe we must work towards, pray towards, and accept that the Church of the twenty-first century will not be a State-Church and prepare our people for that. I think that as far as the Church of England is concerned, it is disintegrating, losing a thousand people a week. Many churches are closing. It is only a matter of time before many more of them will have to close, because their congregations are ageing. Methodists are closing two churches a week in Britain, at the same time as Muslims are opening two mosques a week. That is what is happening in my country. Many of the mosques are former Methodist churches – would you believe it?

Empty church buildings everywhere that were once full of people are becoming furniture stores, youth centres or community clubs. This is a rot that is devastating. However, there are individual churches in the Church of England that are thriving. If you use Alpha Courses, they come from an Anglican church called Holy Trinity Brompton in London, which is really thriving. But it has got twelve million people to draw. The thriving churches are usually in large, urban centres that have a lot of people to draw on. Nevertheless, those churches will survive but they will become free churches. They will simply not be the official Church of England any more.

Of course, when Prince Charles is crowned king (if he is), there will be many religions taking part in the Coronation for the first time. He wants to change one of the titles of royalty: "Defender of the Faith", but few people in England know the history of that title. It was given to Henry VIII for writing a book against Luther, and was given by the Pope. That has continued as a title. It is on our coins – "Defender of the Faith" – but it meant the Roman Catholic faith, not the Protestant, though most people believe it is the latter. But Charles has made it quite clear that he is going to change that title to "Defender of Faith", not "the Faith" but faith, any faith. Charles is advocating Islam now in an open way. One past Prime Minister, Gordon Brown, made a speech in which he said quite openly that Islam is the answer to Britain's problems. You just wonder what is happening.

To address this issue, I wrote a book entitled *The Challenge of Islam to Christians*. When it came out it was regarded with scepticism. Now people are totally different. They ring me up almost daily and say, "It's all coming about just as you said." The inroads they are making are nobody's business. Let me just give you a little personal experience here. I was sitting in a church meeting, minding my own business, and suddenly was overwhelmed with a clear thought which had never occurred to me: that Britain will become an Islamic nation. I sat on it for six months and didn't tell anybody. I didn't even tell my wife. It was almost too much. When you think of your grandchildren, you really wonder what will happen to them.

But anyway, after six months I went to a number of Christian leaders in Britain and consulted them and said, "Look, this is what I've heard in my spirit. What do you think?" Every one of them said, "David, that's of the Lord and you must make it public." I have never had so many people volunteering to stick my neck out, but that is what they did. So, I arranged to do a video of it, and 120 people booked to come, because I like an audience; I am no good at talking to a camera. They booked and we spent three thousand pounds on getting equipment lined up. It was all lined up to do, and just a few days before, I had a stroke and was robbed of my speech. I went through every test imaginable. Brain scan, blood sugar, blood cholesterol—everything absolutely normal. But they said, "Three cranial nerves have been destroyed: the ones that control your throat, your lips, and your tongue." Now you put two and two together. The doctor said, "That should never have happened. There is just no cause for it." But it happened a few days before I was due to give the talk.

Anyway, somebody put that on the internet and asked people to pray that I might be released in my speech. When the day came I was able to speak for five and a half hours and get it all onto a video. But I finished standing on my right leg because my left side was completely out of action. Three men in the front row were leaning forward. I wondered, "What are you doing?" They were ready to catch me; they saw it coming. Anyway, we got it finished and it began to spread the word. Then the book followed, with much more in it.

I really do recommend that you read it. There are now towns in England where whole areas are under Sharia law. It is an extraordinary situation. I get almost weekly information from the inside of Parliament and education authorities, just ringing me up to tell me what is happening in relation to this. So, we are preparing Christians in England for what I believe is the hand of God.

I believe we are in a Habakkuk situation in England. Habakkuk said, "Lord, the state of your people in Jerusalem, what are you doing about it? You're doing nothing, and look at the immorality and idolatry in Jerusalem."

God said, "I am doing something."

"What?"

"I'm bringing the Babylonians."

Habakkuk said, "You couldn't possibly do that because they kill everybody. There'll be nobody left. Your people will be gone."

The Lord said, "The just will survive by keeping faith."

That was Luther's manifesto text I think, but it didn't mean what Luther thought it meant. It meant, "The righteous will not be destroyed; I'll preserve them. They will survive by keeping faith in me." That was the promise.

Now I think God is bringing Islam to Britain. Therefore, I don't tell people, "Let's pray against it." I say, "This is the hand of God. It is a desperate last measure to deal with the weakness of the Church in England." Now that is a pretty tough message. It was for Habakkuk, but I believe it is a message for Britain, and an increasing number of Christians are accepting that as God's word. I have to say that not many church leaders have.

Church leaders are saying, "The real enemy is secularism and we need to unite the three monotheist religions to fight secularism – so we need to become allies with Judaism and Islam to fight secularism." That is extraordinary, because Allah is not the God of the Bible. There are huge differences.

MINISTRY MATTERS

We turn now to the Church's ministry. We have become so used to one-man churches that we take it for granted. But the Holy Spirit has, I think, pointed us in a very different direction. In the very early days of the Pentecostal Church in Norway the leader was asked, "How many members have you now?" I think he said, "Three hundred." The enquirer said, "And how many ministers?" The reply came: "Same number." That is what the Holy Spirit was saying. Alas, many Pentecostal churches have become as much one-man churches as the old-style ones. But the Holy Spirit intends ministry to be shared by all members of the Church.

A friend of mine was a Methodist minister and he wore, as they tend to, a "dog collar", as we call them. He came into his pulpit one Sunday night and preached on the priesthood of all believers. He took as his text Ephesians 4 and said there were some apostles, some prophets, some evangelists, some teachers, and so on. He continued, "Every Christian has a gift and a ministry to do for the Lord." The next Sunday when he came into the pulpit he got a shock. Every one of his members was wearing a dog collar! He said, "Well, what's happening?" He thought he was at synod or something! They said, "You told us we're all in the ministry, and we're just practising what you do." He had never really connected the fact that he dressed differently from all the others with what he was preaching. Well, he never wore the dog collar again.

Do you know it was the Pope in Rome who first criticised his clergy for wearing distinctive dress? The Pope of all people did that because the bishops in France had started wearing special robes because of their position. The Pope said, "You should be distinguished by your character, by your humility, by your compassion, and not by your dress." I have a copy of his letter at home, which I am eagerly showing to people who dress differently. But that is a thing that we have got so used to, and Luther didn't complete his reformation. He left a division between priests and people, which of course was characteristic of the previous thousand years. This division of Christians between professional and lay is a division that you cannot find in the New Testament. It is not of the Lord. It goes back to the Roman Catholic medieval period. Indeed, the white collar was a symbol of your protection by the Virgin Mary in its origin. Most of us are ignorant about its origin.

I am afraid it has been ordination that has made the division between what I call "professional Christians" and "lay Christians". The word "*laos*" in the Greek, which means "people", was applied to everybody in the Church. I am often accused in seminars with the ministers and pastors and priests of trying to abolish the clergy. I say, "You've misunderstood totally. I'm trying to abolish the laity." That is what I am aiming at: to get every Christian into a ministry. So, I want clergy to be the same as members, as in those early Pentecostal days. We are all ministers of one kind or another.

Now that does not mean that the Church does not need leadership. It is very clear in the New Testament that there are some who are called to lead and others who are called to follow. That is not to be confused with ministry. All have a ministry, but those ministries need co-ordination, encouragement, training and leadership. Leadership is in the

New Testament, no question about it. But it is never one-man leadership. It is always corporate leadership. But Church history has drifted from New Testament times, when there were many bishops in each church, to a situation where we have many churches to each bishop.

So that is a complete reversal of the New Testament pattern. The Church of the future, the Church of the twenty-first century, will be a Church in which every member is a minister, but in which there will be corporate leadership—elders. Now of course a *State* Lutheran Church does not have elders, but a Lutheran free church does, I think. That is more in line with the New Testament.

One of the things you cannot do in a one-man church is discipline the membership. If one man tries to discipline a fellowship he is in for very big trouble from his people. But where there is corporate eldership and corporate discipline, a member is up against a group of men and can't blame one man for disciplining them then. It is discipline and doctrine that tend to suffer most in a 'one-man led' church. So as far as ministry goes, there is the priesthood of all believers – Martin Luther taught that. But he didn't practise it. He left this huge division between priest and people intact. I believe we are called to practise it. This idea that *some* are priests is not biblical. We are all priests, and I believe also in the prophethood of all believers. Any believer can be used to speak the word of the Lord to a church.

We had once a month what we called "The Church Business Meeting", but we did the business of the Lord. I asked my wife what she missed most now that we were not leading a church. She said, "I miss the monthly business meeting more than anything else." When she says this to some church people they are utterly astonished. The business meeting to them was fighting, lobbying, voting – the worst kind of democracy. But our business meeting was a theocracy, and any member could bring the word of the Lord, and did so. Do you know the most surprising things came up each month when we asked the Lord, "What do you want us to do," and waited on him? I'll give you just one or two examples. On one occasion a little lady stood up, a very humble little person, but she said, "I believe the Lord wants us to give money to the other churches in the town." Now this was something we had never even thought of doing. We had a huge budget of a hundred thousand pounds a year. We gave a third of that away to the poor, to missionaries, to all kinds of good causes, but to give to other churches in town? Well, they could support themselves. But nevertheless, I went to our bank manager who was called "Julius Caesar". I said, "Mr Caesar, we want to open a new bank account." He said, "Who for?" I replied, "For the other churches in town." He really queried that, but he opened the other bank account. It built up and up until there were hundreds of pounds in it, and we didn't know how to handle it. I mean to go to another church and say, "We'll finance you" – that's terrible. It sounds as if you are taking them over, or making a bid for them, and being patronising towards them. We didn't know what to do with it.

Then a tornado hit our town and took the roof right off the Catholic Church. We said, "Lord, you can't mean this money to go and help them to put the roof back on?" But the Lord said, "I do." I went to the priest of that church and I gave him a huge cheque – enough, pretty well, to put his roof back on. If he'd had a weak heart he'd have been a goner because he staggered back and said, "But, you're the Baptists. I think this must be a world first for Baptists to be supporting the Catholic Church." It wasn't the Charismatic Catholic Church, it was the old one, you know, full of idols and all sorts of things.

This fat Irish priest just couldn't believe it. He said, "Why have you done this?" I said, "Because the Lord told us to." Then he said, "You're the Bible church aren't you?" Now he said that because just a month earlier we had actually read the Bible right through aloud, non-stop, twenty-four hours a day. We decided to do that when we opened our new building to let the whole community know that we stood for the Bible and the whole Bible. So, we simply announced, "We're going to read the Bible through aloud." We had a big chart on the wall, fifteen-minute slots, and anybody could put their name down to read fifteen minutes, but they had to come fifteen minutes earlier to listen to the previous person and stay fifteen minutes after to listen to the next. We were astonished at the result. Two thousand came just to hear the Bible read. We sold half a ton of Bibles over the four days. We read from Sunday night to Thursday morning, around the clock. Men read during the night. Women read during the day. Young people read during the evening.

However, there was a mayor of Guildford who was a little man called "Alderman Sparrow". He really lived up to the name. He said, "I hear you're going to read the Bible right through. I've never heard of such a thing. Could I read as the mayor of the town?" We said, "Yes, but there's only one space left: Tuesday afternoon at three thirty. Could you come for that?" He replied, "Oh yes, I could fit that in. I'll bring my wife." He came. He said, "Do you mind if I wear my chain of office?" I said, "Not at all, it's fine if you wear something else as well." He turned up at the appointed time and asked, "Now what do I read?" I answered, "I don't know. You'll just have to take the Bible and start where they stop."

He read from Proverbs 31, but he hadn't brought his wife. I said, "Where's your wife? You were going to bring her." He said, "Oh, we've got unexpected visitors. She's been up since dawn cooking, cleaning, making the beds. She sends her apologies." Then he just started reading about the ideal wife who gets up at dawn, and looks after.... He could hardly read! Then he read this, "Her husband is well known, for he sits in the council chamber with the other civic leaders." He finished reading, came and sat down by me and said, "I've just been reading about myself in the Bible." I replied, "That's what most people find. They find that the messages here have their name and address on them." Off he went, first saying "Give me a Bible for my wife; I'm going to read this to her."

There was another lady who put her name down. She didn't tell us, but she had an appointment arranged for immediately afterwards, with a lawyer to start divorce proceedings with her husband. Guess what she read? Malachi: "'I hate divorce,' says the Lord." She read this out; she never went to the lawyer, and the marriage is still together. I could give you many stories.... That was just from reading the Bible through!

So, the Catholic priest said, "You're the Bible church, aren't you? You know, my people don't know the Bible. I don't, to tell you the truth. I give them a little talk every Sunday, but would some of your people come and teach my people the Bible?" I said, "I'm sure." We chose a careful team who went and spent a month teaching that church the Bible, and it transformed that church. It all happened because we waited on the Lord, and the Lord said, "Give money to other churches." Every month we had the Lord's business meeting. We waited on the Lord for what he would tell us.

I remember another time he told us, through a very ordinary little man, that we were to give away part of our Sunday evening congregation every Sunday to another church. You had to come forty minutes early to get a seat in our church. Now the Lord was telling us to give our congregation away! So, we would telephone another church and say, "Would you mind if some of our people came to you next Sunday night?" (On Sunday nights they hardly had anybody in their own church – most were Sunday morning people.) We found that our people were being given supper, and were looking forward to getting away from me and hearing someone else. It transformed the town, because now we were the church that was giving to other churches: money and people. None of that would have happened unless we had waited on the Lord and said, "What do you want us to do?"

As I mentioned, my wife misses that monthly meeting more than anything else – when we heard God's orders and did them. It led us into the most astonishing things which we would never have thought of ourselves, because you don't think that way. But the Lord does.

This was a practising ministry involving all members. We had elders who presided at the monthly business meeting. Nevertheless, we had corporate elders. No one of us was above the others. They knew that if the elders said something together, the members needed to take that seriously. But it was not dictatorship, nor was it democracy. It was all of us seeking the Lord together. So, if we wanted a new elder for the church, a name could be put forward by anyone. Usually the elders sought the Lord and brought a name to the people. But we would spend three months praying and thinking about that.

The next monthly meeting that man would not be there and we would discuss him in his absence, fully and frankly, and then a month later, after prayer and discussion, we would ask the people, "Do you recognise this man as your shepherd?" We expected at least eighty percent of the people to say yes. We didn't expect everybody to be in the Spirit; there are always one or two who come with their own mind. But we did expect at least four out of five to say, "We recognise this man as given to us as a shepherd." When the people have shared in that, there is a moral obligation to follow that shepherd because they have shared in the recognition. It was not a democratic vote. We didn't say, "We've got two names and we've got one vacancy, and you can vote on which you put in." That is democracy. We presented one man at a time, having spent three months seeking the Lord, and it was either crystal clear that he was to be the one or it wasn't clear. When it wasn't we said, "Well, we'll wait and see." Sometimes, a year later, they would say, "This man has matured enough to be our shepherd." So, the people shared in every decision of the elders. I am an advocate of open government like that. It is practising the priesthood of all believers. It is believing that anyone in the whole church can minister to the whole church and bring a word of the Lord to the fellowship. We found it worked so beautifully. We didn't have arguments. We didn't have lobbying. We didn't have any of that which is associated so often with the church business meeting. We were practising a theocracy. I am sure that is the right way.

Now I come to the most controversial part: the *membership* of the Church, and here we run into the fact that a state Church is under obligation to accept all its citizens into membership, and to regard all citizens as part of the flock. So that in Norway, for example, there are some three and a half thousand people per parish priest. In Finland, it is lower than that, but you have this allocation of which you are supposed to be the shepherd and they are supposed to be sheep. One of the problems is that a lot of them are goats. A State Church will always result in mixed membership, with a very unclear boundary between Church and world. It means that many people who regard themselves as belonging to the Church are actually no different in lifestyle whatever from those who don't. There is no corporate witness of a different lifestyle because it is such a mixed bag. Now, treating all citizens as part of the flock is to me a delusion, because they are not.

What is the answer to this? Here we get to the big issue.

Baptism marks a boundary of the Church. In the New Testament you are baptised into Christ—into the Head and the Body. Baptism is the sacrament of initiation into the kingdom. I will enlarge on this shortly. But if you baptise babies you are bound to create a mixed church of believers and unbelievers, because there is no guarantee that the baby you baptised will be a strong believer later in life. In fact, the statistics point in the exact opposite direction. I don't know about Norway, but I'd be surprised if it is much different from Finland, where I spoke a while ago. They told me that well over ninety percent of the people have been baptised as babies into the Church, but that less than three percent ever darken the doors on a Sunday. I am not talking about Christmas Eve and specials but about regularly meeting with the Lord's people. That is a huge gap. It is not quite as big in England, but not far off.

So, we have loads of citizens in the State who regard themselves as part of the Church, but who were never in Christ, so that the practice of baptism defines the boundaries of Church membership. That is where the nub of the whole matter is. To cut straight to what I believe, my view is that the churches that survive the twenty-first century will be those which practise New Testament baptism. I will be very blunt now and say that in Norway I find exactly what I find in England and other countries: that *nobody* is preaching and practising New Testament baptism. There are on the whole, three large groups in most countries that I go to in northern Europe. On the one hand are people like Lutherans, Anglicans, and Presbyterians who have, I believe, the right theology of baptism, but the wrong practice. At the other extreme are Pentecostals and Baptists, who have the right practice of baptism, but the wrong theology. I just long to get those two groups together, bang their heads together, and say, "Get back to New Testament baptism." Then there is always a third group, mainly of parachurch organisations from the Salvation Army, Billy Graham Association, Campus Crusade, Navigators, to Youth with a Mission who have deliberately, as a policy, excluded baptism from their evangelism, largely for diplomatic reasons to keep in with the other two groups. Now here is my dilemma: I am a firm believer and advocate for New Testament baptism because I believe it is the answer to the quality of Church membership, which is such a handicap to us still in the twenty-first century. So that we have on the one hand people who have the right preaching about it but the wrong practice, and the right practice but the wrong preaching; and there are also those who don't have either the preaching or the practice. What a situation! Considering that Christ himself put baptism at the heart of his Great Commission, it is an extraordinary situation. He said, "Go and make disciples of all nations, baptising them, and then teaching them to live the way I've commanded." That's his Great Commission. Are any of us doing it?

Let me explain what I mean. I have been on both sides of the fence. I was a Methodist minister for twelve years and I "did" babies. I was always a bit uneasy about it. One day a young lady came to see me and I said, "What can I do for you?" She said, "Well, I'm puzzled about baptism." That lady is now my wife. That was the first conversation we ever had, and it was about baptism, and here we are. She was the first person I ever baptised later, but that is another story.

So, I was one who "did" babies, and then I went out to Arabia when I was a chaplain with the Royal Air Force. My parish extended from Kenya in Africa to Bahrain in the Persian Gulf and inside Saudi Arabia. That was an eye-opener, because every Muslim we baptised was murdered. After a bit I really hesitated to baptise a Muslim, knowing they were signing their death warrant. It is amazing. Others didn't mind them coming to church, or carrying a Bible, or even saying, "I've become a Christian," but the day they were baptised they were murdered. Some of them were knifed. One man we had was burnt. They burned his house down thinking he was in his house, but his wife and children were. They were all burned alive, but he escaped. I have a letter from him at home with his tears blotting the ink telling me about his wife and children being burned alive because he was baptised. I thought, "What is it about baptism that really turns these Muslims on to murder?"

I came to realise that these Muslims had a better understanding of baptism than I had. I had moistened babies' foreheads and given them a name, and it just didn't tie up. I was driven back to my Bible. I looked carefully at all thirty-one passages in the New Testament about baptism – one for each day of the month. I thought, "I can't connect all this with what I'm doing." I came to the conclusion that I should not baptise another baby. Now I had three babies of my own by then, so I had to make the decision for them. But I had to say to the Methodist Church, "I cannot go on doing babies. I'm sorry."

Do you know their reaction? "Will you stay if we give you an assistant to do all the christenings, all the baptisms?" I said, "No, that would be totally dishonest. I'd be preaching baptism in a different way." So, I resigned. They were very reluctant to let me go. I told my wife, "We're going to lose my job, our house, and my pension, and I have nothing else to offer you." I'll never forget what she said: "David, I want to be married to a man who obeys God."

We lost everything overnight, and we lost nothing. We have never lacked anything we needed since. I discovered that my employer was not the Methodist Church but the Lord Jesus Christ, and that he calls you into the ministry of his Body. He doesn't use denominational labels. I have heard thousands of prophecies and in only one was a denominational label mentioned, and it was in New Zealand. The prophecy was given at a big meeting. It was to this effect: "Thus says the Lord, 'I want to bring revival to New Zealand through the Presbyterians.'" I happen to know the man himself was a Presbyterian. I would have been more impressed if a Baptist had said that, but anyway I went to him afterwards and said, "That was a false prophecy. That was from your own heart wish. You'd love to see your denomination lead New Zealand into revival." He accepted that.

But I have never heard the Lord address Lutherans, or Baptists, or Pentecostals. Have you? Never. If the Lord doesn't use these labels, I don't want to, frankly. I actually am a "Method-Bapti-Can" because I have been ordained a Methodist, accredited a Baptist, and I have had Anglican bishops lay hands on me for my travelling ministry. I was waiting for the Pope to come to England to complete the job, but he wasn't interested.

So, I have been on both sides of the baptism issue, and there came a point where I had to say, "I can't do any more babies," because I was so impressed with the New Testament teaching. Now let me be quite frank with you and say I am nearer to Lutherans in the theology of baptism than to Baptists and Pentecostals. But I am nearer to Baptists and Pentecostals in their practice, but certainly not their theology. What is the difference? Well, I have found out that Lutherans, and some Anglicans, emphasise *what God does* in baptism, and emphasise those texts in the New Testament that link baptism to forgiveness of sins, to salvation, to initiation into the Body of Christ. But when that is applied to a baby, the vital conditions for God's activity seem to me to be missing.

Luther himself faced this dilemma, having put all his eggs into the basket of justification by faith. How does that fit baptising a baby? I am sure you are aware of his incredible solution to the dilemma. He said, "Who can say that a baby does not have faith?" To which there is only one logical response: "Who is to say that a baby does?" That was how it was left. So, he kept the medieval practice of baptising babies, but was left with this dilemma. Even more than the question of faith is the emphasis of the New Testament on repentance as a precondition of baptism. Can a baby repent? If they could, what would they repent of? So, there is in all the Lutheran literature I have read about baptism a complete absence of any discussion of repentance in relation to it.

I am convinced from scripture that God really *does* something in baptism; that it is not a symbolic act, it effects what it symbolises. It is both a bath and a burial. Ananias said to Paul, or Saul of Tarsus as he was then, "What are you waiting for? Rise and be baptised and have your sins washed away, calling on his name." That is a very high view of baptism: "And have your sins washed away." Peter has the same very high view when he says, "Baptism now saves you, not by washing dirt from your body but by an appeal to God for a clean conscience through the resurrection of Jesus." When you put all these texts together it is saying that it is a means of grace; that it is a channel for God to do something for you that nothing else could do. I put it very simply: to give you a clean start in your Christian life by washing the sins not off heaven's record, but off your conscience.

I am going to tell you a few real-life stories from my own experience to illustrate this, just to give you the feel of where I am. First, we had a man in our church called Roger, a consultant engineer who, whenever he had to go away as a consultant, to go and visit another city, always took a woman from that city to bed. He never told his wife about this. Every time he left home he was unfaithful to her. Well, both Roger and his wife came to faith in Christ almost at the same time. He came to me shortly afterwards and said,

"David, I just can't live with it. I've told my wife everything. I've confessed my guilt, my infidelity to her, but I can't look her in the eye. She sits opposite me at the breakfast table and I can't look her in the face. I'm so ashamed of what I did. It's unbearable."

I said, "You know what you need? Baptism." I took him to that text in 1 Peter where it says that it doesn't wash dirt from your body, but it gives you a clean conscience through the resurrection. I baptised him and his wife together. I baptised the wife, and she went up out of the pool dripping wet and stood there waiting for him. Roger, when he went down into the water, yelled out at the top of his voice, "Lord Jesus, wash my conscience clean." He came up out of the water, the other side, and he ran to his wife, and he held her and looked her in the eye and said, "I'm a different man." Baptism had cleansed his conscience. From then on, he always talked about his past as if it was someone else, the old man who had been buried in baptism. He was a new man now — clean in God's sight.

I baptised the singer Cliff Richard, who was a member of our congregation. He has written in his autobiography, "David Pawson washed me, rinsed me, and hung me up to dry, and I never felt so clean in all my life." That is what baptism did for him.

Another young man in the town in which I lived was a Hell's Angel. He was into drugs, motorbikes and the lot and he had on his chest a tattoo of Satan. There was the devil tattooed on him. He knew when he came to Christ that he should be baptised, but he didn't want to be because he noticed that your shirt went transparent in the water. He didn't want anybody to see the devil on his body. So, he kept putting it off. Finally, he went to our local hospital in Basingstoke and got hold of a plastic surgeon. He said, "Could you remove this tattoo from my body, because I want to be baptised?" The surgeon said, "Well I can. There are two ways. One is to burn it off, and that will leave a big scar. The other is to take a skin graft from your thigh and transplant it in the place of what we remove up here. But that costs an awful lot of money; you can't get that on the National Health Service, and it'll take months." The young man said, "Oh, I can't wait, and I haven't the money."

So, he asked a friend of mine to baptise him, which he did in a swimming pool in the garden of a member in Basingstoke. There were Christians around the pool. He went down into the water to bury his past and to wash away his sins, and he came up out of the water without that tattoo. Gone—a tattoo washed by H_2O with God in it! If you tell him that baptism is just a symbol he will laugh at you. He'll say, "Baptism took the devil off me."

Here is one more story—and I could give you hundreds. A friend of mine is a Baptist minister in North London. At school he had been a close friend with another boy, but when they left school they parted and lost touch with each other, as often happens. Neither of them were Christians. But one of those boys, my friend, became a believer and eventually found himself pastor of a Baptist church. The other youngster went the wrong way, down and down. He got into drugs, got into crime, and got into everything bad you can imagine. Finally, at the age of about twenty-three or four he became suicidal and decided to end it all. Then he remembered his friend from school. He thought, "I wonder where he is. I feel if I could just get through to him he could help me."

He didn't know how to find this friend from school, so he went to a spiritist medium and said, "Could you tell me where my friend from school is?" She went into a trance and she came out of the trance and she said, "I can describe for you the house he lives in." She described the house in detail. She said, "It's opposite a big park with trees," and gave detail after detail. But she said, "I can't give you the address but I think it's in North London somewhere" – and North London is a pretty big place. But then she said, "I've got bad news for you. He died a few years ago." The young man was so desperate he wouldn't believe that. He set off and spent weeks searching North London. He finally found a park with trees and he found the exact house she had described in the trance. He went up and knocked at the door and his friend from school answered the door and led him to the Lord, saved his life, and he has got his life together now, in Christ.

But this young man, who is now a lovely Christian, said to my friend, "But she told me you were dead and she gave me the date of your death." My friend, the Baptist pastor said, "What date was that?" He gave it to him. He said, "That was the day I was baptised." So, baptism cuts you off from the demonic world. That is my conclusion. Just as baptism in the Red Sea cut the Israelites off from Pharaoh, and I have got biblical warrant for that analogy – I believe that baptism is an operation of God.

Now that is why I have quarrels with the Baptists and Pentecostals as well. Because they never talk about what *God* does in baptism; it is all about what man does: either an act of obedience to the Lord or an act of testimony to other people, a kind of "wet witness", but there is no talk about what God does for the believer. Do you see what I am getting at? I want to see all that put together biblically – a belief in New Testament baptism that actually does wash away sins, that actually does incorporate you into Christ, that actually does save you, but when it is applied to a repenting, believing candidate. That is where I have come to. So, I am afraid I find myself in no man's land, between those who have the right understanding of it but do it to the wrong people, and those who do it to the right people but don't have any understanding of what God does. Let us get it together.

I believe that a recovery of New Testament baptism would be one of the biggest changes we could make that would do something for the Church that nothing else would do. I am passionate about this because I really believe that would cure so many of our problems. It would mean a Church of penitent believers only, and a Church that could then be in a position to be called to a new lifestyle—a holy Church. I believe it would also be a means of grace to the new believer – that baptism should be part of initiation into life in the kingdom, and not shuttered off into a church ceremony or other things. At last we could evangelise as Jesus told us to, and make disciples of all nations, baptising them and teaching them how to live the Christian life. That is his mandate.

Oh, if only we could get back to that, and do it all together, and get the Lutheran understanding of what baptism is and does, and what God does in it, together with the Baptist and Pentecostal understanding of doing it only to repentant believers. I believe then we would be back to New Testament baptism. I believe God would honour that and would really use it to do wonders for the Church. But it requires courage on the part of those who feel that this is important. I had to resign from the Methodist ministry. It cost us everything, and yet it cost us nothing. But God has honoured that more than I could possibly say.

I am giving all the glory to the Lord for what I am going to mention now. But at this moment I have the largest ministry I have ever had. I am able to minister in 120 countries. Everybody in China can get my teaching on television. Scientists at the South Pole are watching my Bible videos every week. And here I am—a nobody; I have no organisation, no office, no secretary. I write my letters and books with a pen. I don't have a computer; I'm not on email. I don't even have a mobile phone. People think I have come out of Noah's Ark. Yet the Lord has taken this simple person and given me a worldwide ministry such as I could never have dreamt of, and I have never done anything to seek that. I have never advertised anything. I have never asked anybody to distribute my material. But we now have a circle of worldwide distributors, in every one of the six continents, and I have done nothing for that. I have simply given the Lord my mouth and said, "I want to teach your Word and the whole Word," and he has opened the doors for us. We have done absolutely nothing to get that. I just hand that to you. I must have got something right for the Lord to do that, but I date it back to the day I said, "I'm not going to do any more babies." From that day, the Lord began to use me in a wider way than ever before.

I am not trying to prove anything to you and I am not trying to persuade you. But I make a plea: let us get back to New Testament baptism and put it at the centre of our evangelism where Jesus meant it to be. It gives a new believer the best start he or she could have in the Christian life, coupled with praying for the baptism in the Spirit after that. Every new believer needs both baptisms. That is the third major thing that I believe the Church needs reformed, but it is going to take tremendous conviction and courage to achieve that, and it will be at great cost because we are up against vested interest.

The next thing I want to mention regarding the Church is the matter of discipline. Luther said that this was one of the marks of the true Church. Yet in the average church today there is no discipline whatever. I will tell you this, and you can make what you like of it. Increasingly, the churches are led by women, and they find discipline difficult. That is why I believe that in the family the father has been given the responsibility of discipline, not the mother. In the Church, I believe it takes men to discipline the Church.

The more feminised the Church is, the less disciplined it seems to become. So many ordained women today are pressing for homosexual marriage and other things. That is not a coincidence, because women respond with their hearts. We can separate mind and heart as men, and therefore we can be more objective in dealing with people's feelings. But that is another story.

I want to tackle the biggest question of discipline in my thinking in the Church today, which is not homosexuality. I believe that we prepared the way for this in the sixties by compromising on one issue: divorce and remarriage. I believe that the Church that compromised on that issue is a Church that has laid itself open to all the questions we are now facing today in a crisis. The Church of England is facing a major crisis, and it is a question of whether it can hold together now with the African bishops on the one hand and the American bishops on the other, completely at loggerheads.

In a word, I believe scripture tells us absolutely clearly that remarriage after divorce is out, and that Christ made a clear stand there in his teaching, that the Church is now widely ignoring or deliberately disobeying and adapting to modern culture. It was back in the sixties when this happened. I was on a special commission by the Evangelical Alliance in Britain, chaired by John Stott, to debate the new legislation that was coming in, whereby divorce could be on the ground of marriage breakdown, not any other, and that Britain would recognise that a marriage had broken, and therefore could be dissolved. Christians were then faced with whether they stood by Jesus' teaching or went along with new legislation. It was that particular issue that I believe began to destroy the discipline of the Christian Church in Britain.

So, we had varying responses. For the most part, the free churches were prepared to marry the innocent party in a divorce. The Anglican Church was not prepared to remarry, but has blessed remarriages. I for one cannot understand how we can ask God to bless a remarriage and yet be unwilling to conduct it. That seems to me hypocrisy. But there we are. It is totally inconsistent. The Roman Catholic Church has greatly increased what it calls "annulment of marriage" and finds some reason for declaring that a marriage was not a marriage at all in the first place. So, they have taken their own line to this. But right across the board we have the fact that the majority of Christian churches in my country, in one way or another, are now blessing remarriage after divorce.

Leading Christian evangelists, pastors, and Bible teachers are now openly changing wives and justifying it by saying, "My new wife is a much better partner in my ministry than the old one was." It is quite incredible. I could name names that you know and would recognise, of foremost Christian evangelists and leaders in my country who have simply divorced their wife and married someone else, usually an associate in the work, or a secretary, or somebody working closely with them. I am openly speaking to that situation and making myself terribly unpopular for doing so, but I simply preach what Christ taught.

But having opened that door, I give you some figures from America. At first it was liberals who began to lower the standards of the sanctity of marriage. Then it became evangelicals. The situation now in America is that the "Bible Belt", as it is known, in the southern USA where the Southern Baptists (who are known as Bible believers), are the major denomination, now has a higher divorce rate – fifty percent higher than the rest of America. And that is where the Bible is widely respected. Not only that, but eighty percent of all juvenile delinquency or child crime comes from broken homes and ended marriages. That is true of my country. We now have the highest divorce and remarriage rate in Europe.

It is right among the evangelical and Bible believers. They are changing partners like that.

Well once the Church, as it were, reduced the sanctity of marriage in the sixties by going along with the idea that marriage could be dissolved and replaced, then all the other gender issues began streaming in behind that. We now face the biggest gender issue of all: will the Church marry homosexuals? I turned on the television (the BBC) for a service of worship from a church in Somerset. Here was a minister "marrying" or pronouncing a "blessing" on two men in the name of Jesus. I honestly felt sick in my stomach. Then there was another church in the same county where in one service the minister "dissolved" a marriage of a couple in his church and in the name of Jesus said, "You are now free and separate." In the same service he married the man to another woman in his congregation (or performed a "blessing") and "married" the woman to another woman in the congregation—a former nun (or, again, gave a "blessing"). All this in the name of Jesus in a Christian church, but I am sorry, that is where we are. This is going to be a great pressure on us: whether we are going to be pressured by the State into a complete denial of the sanctity of marriage.

In Jesus' teaching, nothing dissolves a marriage except death. That should be, I believe, our stand. The exceptions that he made are both in Matthew for a reason, because Matthew is a Jewish Gospel written for Jews—for the early Jewish believers. The exception is due to Jewish culture. The word he used was not "adultery" but "fornication". When the word "fornication" (*porneia*) is used in the same context as "adultery" (*moicheia*), they are clearly two different things. Jesus does that, and so does Paul in many of his references. Fornication is sex before marriage. Adultery is sex after marriage with someone else. The only exception

Jesus made was fornication, not adultery. But even the New International Version has changed that word to "marital unfaithfulness", which is unwarranted mistranslation. In Jewish culture, betrothal or engagement is far more serious than in our culture. Engagement can be broken in our culture. But in Jewish culture, that is as good as the promises made in a wedding. Therefore, if the bridegroom discovers that his bride has already had sex before they are married he is totally at liberty to divorce her. The word "divorce" there is in an engagement context, not a marriage context.

Of course, Matthew also gives us a classic example of that with Mary and Joseph, where Joseph had not consummated marriage with Mary, but believed that she had already fornicated with someone else, so resolved to divorce her. That would have been the right thing to do. He was a just and a righteous man. But an angel told him the whole truth and said, "You don't need to be afraid of taking her as your wife; she has not been unfaithful to you. The child is by the Holy Spirit." That example, in the same Gospel as the two exceptions, tells you the context. In a Jewish culture, a man was almost bound to put away his intended wife if she was found to be fornicating beforehand.

In Matthew 5, Jesus simply said that a man who gets rid of his wife is forcing her into adultery and is responsible for that, except if he divorces her for being unfaithful before the marriage—for fornication. Therefore, I am convinced that based on a careful reading of Jesus' words, his teaching made no exceptions. In Mark and Luke, written for Gentile unbelievers, there is no mention of any exception whatsoever, because there isn't the same Jewish culture of the binding betrothal from which there should and could be divorce before the marriage.

The Church went soft on divorce and remarriage, and it is now happening not just among members but also among ministers. All over, wherever I go, I find this. In Jesus' eyes it is legalised adultery. As soon as the Church gave way on the sanctity of marriage the other things swept in. In the same way, in the sixties the Church gave way on the sanctity of life by supporting the abolition of capital punishment, which the Lord laid on us in the Noahic Covenant, which was made with all mankind, and which God has kept, but we haven't—that a murderer deserves to die and his life must be taken. When we abolished that in the sixties I predicted then, "This is the end of the sanctity of life," and therefore murder is no longer sacrilege, the destruction of God's image. I said, "The new thing will be abortion, and the thing after that will be euthanasia." Once you have taken one step to reduce the sanctity of life, all these other things follow. So, we are now battling with abortion and we are battling with potential euthanasia.

In the sixties, two sacred things were reduced: the sanctity of life and the sanctity of marriage. The result is what we are now grappling with and being crippled by today. But I just want to show you that it all began then. We are now reaping the harvest and being put in such pressurised situations. The Church – if it doesn't marry homosexuals – will be under persecution from the authorities. That will be regarded as treason, as anti-citizenship. I tell you that now. We as Christian leaders will have to decide whether we are going to compromise or not on these crucial issues. It is going to be very costly to stand firm by the commandments of Jesus. He said, "Go and make disciples of all nations, baptising them and teaching them to observe all that I have commanded you." Among those commandments is his clear teaching on the sanctity of life and the sanctity of marriage, that in God's sight must never be broken.

The discipline of the Church is now suffering because we compromised back in the sixties without realising what we were doing. We were making ourselves vulnerable to pressure from the political and social authorities to do what they want. Friends of mine, a couple in the West Country, have been in the national press. Every paper in Britain has had their photograph printed because they have fostered twenty-eight children who didn't have a home. Each child they have brought up as their own and they have really saved these kids from what they would have become because of the bad homes the children came from. Three months ago, they were told, "You must sign a paper to approve children being adopted by homosexual couples or you cannot foster any more children for us." They said, "We cannot sign that paper." The boy that they were bringing up as their own right then was immediately taken from them and put in another foster home. This hit the headlines of every newspaper in Britain. This dear Christian couple had refused to sign that paper from the council and therefore were immediately removed from all fostering of children who needed a home. It caused a huge storm of course, but I am afraid it is just another straw on the water indicating the way the stream is going.

I have mentioned the State Church, I have mentioned ministry, I have mentioned membership and the related issue of baptism and I have mentioned discipline.

Finally, I was asked this question: would I tell remarried people who discovered this to divorce? I believe that anybody living in sin must repent. "Repent" means turning away from that. If they are in an adulterous relationship of any kind, repentance means leaving that relationship. I take my hat off to couples I know who separated when they realised that they were living in adultery in the sight of the Lord. We can only tell them to repent and warn them that the cost of not repenting could be eternal.

TYING UP LOOSE ENDS

The question of baptism is of course the hot issue. I spoke about it to an audience of eight thousand from all over Finland. The recordings of my talks in Finland were banned because the sponsors of the meeting were Lutheran, but somebody had managed to get one and was selling it on the black market for an exorbitant price. Then somebody else put a copy on the internet, and so they withdrew the ban on my recordings and let them go. The Lutherans challenged me to go back for a public debate with professors of theology on baptism—a debate that would be televised. It was an extraordinary situation; I won't go into details. But it began when I was told that out of 180 minutes I would be allowed one! I said, "I'm not coming." They said, "Well, four." I said, "No way." They said, "Six and a half," out of 180 minutes. I said, "No way. Fifteen minimum." They said, "Well ten." I said, "Fifteen." They said, "Thirteen." I am not exaggerating; this is what went on with the man who was going to chair the debate. Anyway, I was getting very frustrated. I could see they just were not going to let me speak. They even said this to me: "You realise you'll be up against educated men." I thought, "The implications of that are not very flattering!" Anyway, I was relieved because Channel 7, which is a widely watched channel on television in Finland, said to me, "We'll give you an hour and twenty minutes separately on television, just for you to give your understanding." So, I went into the public debate feeling, "You don't know it, but I've got an hour and twenty minutes for my views on the television." A DVD has been made available of those two programmes which I made for Finnish television, meeting the points that were made in the debate. In fact, I did get the chance to expand on the debate.

The last two points I want to make concern, firstly, church life, and secondly, Israel. I believe the Church of the twenty-first century must relate to Israel and to the Jewish people. It is extraordinary as I go around, how the promise made to Abraham is being fulfilled in church after church. "Whoever blesses your descendants will be blessed and whoever curses you will be cursed." Of course, the Jewish people are not just those who are in Israel today. That is only less than half of the Jews in the world. Unfortunately, in this matter Martin Luther has left us a terrible legacy. Wherever Lutheranism has gone, anti-Semitism has followed. The Church has been generally guilty of appalling anti-Semitism.

We had a lady in our church, a Jewish lady from Vienna, and when she was a little girl, whenever she walked past a church on Sunday, the people coming out would kick her, spit on her, and say, "You killed Jesus." This little Jewish girl said, "Well I had nothing to do with that." She became very bitter as a child. Happily, the Holy Spirit was able to heal that, she became a wonderful Christian and had an amazing influence on other Jewish people, helping them to get rid of their bitterness against the Christian Church. Our record of anti-Semitism is terrible.

Martin Luther began, as you probably know, very sympathetic towards Jewish people. He honestly believed that now he had got rid of all the Catholic practices which appeared to be idolatry, and which the Jews had used to criticise the Catholic Church, they would now welcome his New Testament Christianity, which he believed was much nearer biblical Judaism. After all, Jesus was, is, and always will be a Jew. So, he tried to evangelise the Jews in Germany, and they wouldn't have it. He became at first disappointed, then frustrated, and then very angry and hostile, and became the worst anti-Semite in Protestant history.

He wrote an article or a booklet entitled "The Jews and their Lies", and he advocated a seven-stage programme to rid Germany of the Jews. I read the seven stages: "Their synagogues must be burned down, their houses demolished, their books confiscated, their rabbis silenced or executed, their passports withdrawn so they cannot escape, their money lending forbidden, and put all of them to hard labour to drive these rascally lazybones out of our system." That was Luther's programme. His final sermon before he died was preached against the Jews and in it he pleaded with Germany to get rid of them. Thank God he died two or three days later before he expanded on the theme.

That is the legacy he left, which is a good deal worse than Catholic anti-Semitism. I don't know if you heard about Kristallnacht, the night when the Jewish shop windows of Berlin were smashed and the synagogues burned. That was on Luther's anniversary, and Hitler himself said, "I am doing the Lord's will," and appealed to Luther for support. It is a shameful episode in Church history. Therefore, it led directly to the Holocaust in Germany. Hitler was appealing to Luther to justify that ethnic cleansing.

Well, I say no more except that I believe the Church needs to repent of its anti-Semitism of centuries. I regularly speak in synagogues as well as churches, by their invitation. I don't pull any punches; I always talk about Yeshua, Jesus Christ, Ha-Mashiach (the Messiah). I never hide that. They know perfectly well I am a Christian, but I try to talk about him in such a way that they don't associate him with the Church's history.

Unfortunately, many parts of the Christian Church have been so horrified by the Holocaust that they have gone to an opposite extreme: mainline denominations in the Western world are now saying, "Let's stop trying to convert Jews. Let's not proselytise them." The teaching is now officially called the "double covenant teaching": that the Jews are saved by their own covenant, and Christians are saved by the new covenant, and we must not try and lead them to Yeshua Ha-Mashiach. They are saved by God their way and we are saved our way. That is the new relativism translated from the guilt complex that the Holocaust left in so many Christian hearts. There were people, however, like the Sisters of Darmstadt who have repented on behalf of Germany, and who have nevertheless maintained that the Jewish people need a Saviour—their Messiah.

I would go every year to Jerusalem for the Feast of Tabernacles, but one year we ran into problems. Seven thousand Christians from 120 countries gathered, the biggest number ever. At one of the events we marched through Jerusalem and tried to contact Israelis. However, this year the Chief Rabbinate in Jerusalem, which is the headquarters of world Judaism, forbade any Jew to have anything to do with us Christians. Of course, that meant that we had to cancel one night when we invariably invite hundreds of Jews to be our guests. They gladly come, including the Prime Minister who usually comes. This time, Ehud Olmert sent a video recorded message to us. But when chief rabbis tell Jews not to do something, you know what happens. They are stiff-necked people still, and they do it. Eighty thousand Israelis turned out to greet the Christians on the march, which was a bigger crowd than ever. However, the International Christian Embassy, who organised the feast, was criticised for inviting two people to speak: Jack Hayford and myself. The Chief Rabbi had got hold of tapes of my talks and those of Jack Hayford (who wrote the chorus "Majesty"). Parts of what we had said were quoted and we were accused of believing that Jews were not saved until they had met the one we claim to be the Messiah – which is what Jack and I both believe, and we stand for. We don't hide it. But we realise that we have got to overcome centuries of fear of Christians before we can really get through, because Jews have very long memories, and the crusades were like yesterday to them.

I believe that now the Church must not only repent of its anti-Semitism but develop a theology of Israel that combines their future with ours. Romans chapter 11 alone is enough to tell us that our God has not finished with the Jewish people and has a future planned for them, a future that is tied up with our future. I have noticed as I travel that the Lord is blessing churches that are blessing Israel; and yet those who are still anti-Semitic, or at least by default are ignoring the Jewish people, are still praising, funnily enough, the God of Israel. For the God of Israel is our God; he is the Father of Jesus.

This is a dimension of Church life which I believe will characterise flourishing churches in the twenty-first century: a recovery of a theology of Israel. A detailed consideration of the five covenants of scripture is beyond the scope of this book, but it is important to realise that this is a covenantal issue. We are not under the Mosaic covenant, but the Abrahamic covenant, the Davidic covenant and the Noahic covenant (made with Noah) are all reaffirmed in the New Testament as still standing. Of course, Abraham, Isaac and Jacob are not dead. They are still alive. God's covenant with them is still valid. That is the basis of their claim to the Promised Land. I believe anybody who believes the Word of God must accept that God has brought the Jews back to their Promised Land.

Do you believe that God is sovereign over history, that he controls the Babylonians, the Egyptians and the Assyrians as well as the Jews, that he brought the Philistines from Crete to the Promised Land at the same time as he brought the Jews? Amos tells us that it is God who is sovereign over history. As Paul said in his speech on Mars Hill in Acts 17, God decides how much time and how much space any nation has in the world. If you believe that, then the fact is the Jews are back in the Promised Land.

If you believe that God is sovereign over all history you believe that God must have brought them back. It is too extraordinary a thing: after two thousand years without their language, without their finance, without their land, they are back in it and are flourishing as no other nation is flourishing today. It is an extraordinary situation, and yet of course they are also, humanly speaking, under threat of extinction. Middle East crises are affecting the entire world, and the world is now believing that if there can be peace in the Middle East there can be peace in the world. It has become the hinge of history.

All that is another big subject. But I believe that Christians should let the New Testament decide their attitude to the Jewish people, not the Old. We are often accused as Christian Zionists of living in the Old Testament. I don't; I live in the New. But there is enough in the New Testament to make me a Zionist and to make me back Israel. I do not support Israel right or wrong. I am one of their biggest critics because I believe a real friend does not approve everything. I have seriously criticised them publicly for aborting a million and a half of their own babies since 1948. That is the same number that were butchered in the gas ovens of Germany – children.

Their biggest crisis is that by 2020 there will be more Arab Muslims in Israel than Jews. It is a demographic crisis for them. Either many more Jews will need to go back and boost the numbers, or the parents already there will have to have bigger families like the Muslims, and will not have to practise the abortion or even birth control (as they have been) to solve that one. So, they have huge problems. Humanly speaking, you would not put your money on Israel surviving in the twenty-first century.

But I believe God has decided that already, and that we need to enlarge our theology of Israel and understand that the God we worship every day is the God of Israel, and that Jesus was, is, and always will be a Jew, and that a Jew will one day be King of the world. Now all that is quite revolutionary, but it is a further mark of the Church in the twenty-first century that it will be concerned with the Jewish people and will preach and practise that God has a united destiny for us both: one new man in Christ forever, one flock under one shepherd.

The final note, I believe, is that we need to reform our eschatology: our hope about the future. Faith, hope, and love are the three dimensions of Christian living. Faith essentially relates to the past work of God. Love relates to the present work and people of God. But hope relates to the future work of God. We live in a world that is increasingly without hope. At the beginning of the twentieth century, the word on everybody's lips was "progress". Everybody believed that the twentieth century was going to be the healthiest, happiest, wealthiest, safest century of all. It was the sinking of the Titanic that pricked that bubble. That was its significance. It was the first major challenge to human optimism in the twentieth century. It was the largest moving object man had ever made. It was the highest technical object of its day. It was the supreme achievement of scientific humanism. It went down on the maiden voyage. The ship which they said "God himself could not sink" went down. From then on, the optimism that had begun the century, the optimism that had led a British Prime Minister to coin the slogan, "Up and up and up and on and on and on", which won him an election, was widely held.

Soon after the Titanic came World War I, and the sheer horror of the blood and mud of the trenches in Belgium and France. It seemed impossible, and you know it killed the faith of thousands of men who had been Christians before that war. Many were killed physically, but even more were killed spiritually and said, "How can there be a God of love and all this happening?" because it was the most barbaric war ever. The result was that churches in Britain lost their men. From then on churches in Britain became what I call "lifeboat churches" – women and children first. Women were leading the Church and carrying the Church. The men did not come back to Church after World War One. They said, "We've seen and done things that we just cannot line up with the God that the Church told us existed." So, it was a major national disaster.

The word on everybody's lips as we opened the twenty-first century was not "progress" but "survival". It is a question now: "Will the human race survive this century?" Scientists have already given us the date by which human life will begin to be impossible on earth and the date is 2040. That comes from the Massachusetts Institute of Technology where they have fed into a computer all the trends. Oil being consumed, fresh water available, population explosion; they have fed all the factors in and have announced that by 2040 human life will become impossible in great areas on Earth. Now you may live to see that; I certainly won't. But that is the date that the new science of futurology (as it is called) is giving us.

There is, I find, an attitude of almost despair, or hopelessness, even in Christian congregations. I now check them and I say, "I'm going to ask you to vote on whether you believe this century will be better than the twentieth, the same, or worse." Many expect it to be much worse. Indeed, based on my experience of asking this question, a typical vote of a Christian congregation would come down on the side of it getting worse. But the result of such a vote would have been completely reversed if I had been alive to ask that in 1900. That is the change of mood. People are therefore more existential, living for the present, because they fear the future.

It is against that backcloth we have a solemn obligation to tell the world about the Christian hope. "Hope" in English is a very ambiguous word. "I hope the weather will be like this tomorrow." "I hope we'll have a good holiday." "I hope they can sort out some of the problems." This means simply, "I'd like to think it would." It is not a certainty. Whereas the Greek word *elpis*, in the New Testament, means what you are absolutely sure is going to happen. This is the hope that we have, and which we alone have, because the only people who know how the world is going to end are Christians – we have a Bible that tells us.

I don't know if you realise that the Bible has 735 *different* predictions about the future. Some of them are made many times. One of them is made over 300 times. I am not trying to blind you with statistics. What a horrible word that is! (One of my ancestors coined the term.) You can prove anything with statistics, I know, but I am giving you figures. Of 735 predictions about the future in the Bible, 596 have already come true after the prediction, in detail. That is eighty-one percent that have already happened – to the letter. I am prepared to believe the rest. It doesn't take a lot of faith on my part to believe the rest will happen; the other nineteen percent are all about the end of the world. They obviously have not happened yet or we would not be here. That is an amazing record. Superstitious ways of finding the future like from tea leaves, tarot cards or whatever are never more than five percent right. Yet there isn't a daily tabloid newspaper that would come out without an astrology column but they have never been more than five percent right, or as I put it, "ninety-five percent wrong."

The new science of futurology, which now has its own professors, has never been more than twenty-five percent right in extrapolating the present trends into the future because there are always unexpected events that change the future. Therefore, as I say, seventy-five percent wrong. The Bible hasn't been eighty-one percent right, because those predictions of the nineteen percent could not yet have happened. It has been one hundred percent accurate up till now. Therefore, it doesn't take a leap of faith for me to say that the other nineteen percent are going to happen exactly as predicted.

I would love to take you through some of these astonishing predictions. The prediction about Tyre, that it would be thrown into the sea, has never happened to any city in history, but to Tyre it happened. Ezekiel said it would happen long before it did, but it was Alexander the Great who threw the entire city into the sea to make a causeway out to the island where the inhabitants fled. So Ezekiel's word was fulfilled to the letter – an entire city, sticks, stones, bricks, everything, thrown into the sea. It has never happened since to any other city, but it happened to Tyre as Ezekiel said it would.

I believe that this is the current mood in the Church – in this atmosphere of fear of the future, of despair almost, of depression certainly, and the existentialism that results from wanting to live for the now, to live for today and what you can squeeze out of today before the stock markets collapse, before the economy goes haywire; live for today; spend it now. Indeed, get as much credit as you can now so you can get a much bigger house than you can afford. You know what that leads to. We suffered a major crisis in Britain because of the American debts for houses. Enough said.

We have a message of hope; we have a message of the future. Now at this point I want to say that we need a biblical philosophy of history. Perhaps you did not even know there was one, but I am going to spell it out. Once again, Luther misled in this by decrying the book of Revelation. Yet it is in the Bible. It is part of the Word of God. It is the one book in the New Testament that deals with the future and it is a book that many preachers and churches have ignored—just quoting little bits of it. But we need to grasp the whole of it because there is a whole philosophy of history. What do I mean by that phrase? I mean the shape of future events—the pattern. Historians have been trying for centuries to discern whether there is a pattern in history that can make sense of the kaleidoscope of events. There have been at least five major philosophies of history which are adopted in the mass media and are fed to us indirectly every day. If we are not careful we adopt a worldly philosophy of history and forget the biblical, which is one reason why people who are soaked in the Bible don't fall for worldly philosophies.

Here are the five. The first is the *circular* philosophy of history — that history goes around in circles. You just keep going back on yourself, and the same thing happens again and again. This was the Greek pattern of history. Life is a roundabout. You'll get off much where you got on. Nothing has happened. You have made no progress. A common proverb in English is "history repeats itself". That is the circular view of history: round and round, going nowhere.

The second view is called the *cyclic* view of history. This says that history is moving forward, but it is moving forward in an up and down motion. There are triumphs and tragedies, boom and bust, inflation and deflation; history has this pattern and will go on having this pattern until it ends.

Whether it ends on an up or a down is anybody's guess. It is not going back on itself, nor is it always going forward to something new, but it is up and down. I am simplifying all this just to give you a summary in your mind.

Third is the *pessimistic* view of history. This is that history just goes down and down and down, gets worse and worse and worse. That is a very common philosophy of history today.

Then there is the fourth view, an *optimistic* view of history, which was more characteristic a hundred years ago, that goes like this: up and up and up and on and on and on. That was born out of Darwin's theory of evolution, the idea that there is constant progress upwards to higher things.

Against all those, the Bible has a unique philosophy of history which we call the *apocalyptic* view of history. This is shared by communists, Jews, and Christians. They all got it from the same source: the Hebrew prophets. To draw this one is to go down and down and down, and suddenly up, and then maintain the line on a higher level than ever. So, you have this kind of pattern. That is the communist's view of history. Karl Marx was Jewish and he got it from the Jewish prophets and from his Jewish background. It is the philosophy of history in all the Old Testament prophets. It is the view of history in the New Testament.

The only difference between the three is what causes that sudden upthrust to a higher level than ever before. For the communist it is the revolution, when the bourgeoisie finally take over from the proletariat and we get a new utopia, which is classless and crimeless. Of course, it is a dream that has now been shattered. Russia is now way away from that. They thought it would bring in the utopia; it didn't. The Jews say it will come when God breaks into history and brings the kingdom of God to earth. The Christian is very near to that, but takes it one step further and says, "That will happen when the King comes, when the Messiah comes to establish the rule of God on earth." That is the difference.

So, we have this apocalyptic view of history and we need to teach our people this so that when it happens they are not surprised or shocked. When things do get worse and worse they know it is all part of a pattern and that they can look forward to a sudden uplift when the King comes back, and then life reaches a higher level than ever before. This philosophy of history is realistic. It is not pessimistic because it does not think it is going to go on and on and down forever. But it is not optimistic about the immediate future. Christian hope looks to the ultimate future, not to the immediate future. It looks right ahead.

That apocalyptic philosophy of history, I find, is not being taught in churches. We have come under the influence of, on the one hand, creeds, especially the Nicene Creed, which was the result of Constantine's first calling a Council together in northwest Turkey. The creeds say he is coming back to judge the living and the dead. Therefore his coming back does not arouse a hope, an optimism in a congregation reciting a creed. In my Bible, the Last Judgment does not take place when Jesus comes back to earth. Indeed, it only comes after the earth has passed away. So he is not coming back to judge the earth. Even if the creed says that, scripture doesn't. It says that the earth and heaven will pass away and only then will the Great White Throne of Judgment appear.

So, every Christian believes Jesus is coming back, but the real question is: why? We know *how* he is coming back: the same way he went, with clouds. We know *where* he is coming back. The Bible is quite clear. He is coming back to Jerusalem, the same place he left. We don't know when he is coming back, though I believe I can tell you the month, even if I cannot tell you the year, because Jesus always did things according to the Jewish calendar.

The one of the three great feasts he has not fulfilled is the Feast of Tabernacles. The Jewish expectation of the Messiah is at the Feast of Tabernacles. Old Testament and the New Testament both tell us exactly this. It is why (in John chapter 7), his brothers said to Jesus, "You think you're the Messiah? Why don't you go up to the Feast of Tabernacles and show them?" He said, "My time has not come yet," and went up secretly. If you read Luke's Gospel carefully you find that Jesus was born not on December 25th, but during the Feast of Tabernacles—late September or early October. The evidence is there for you to see. It is wonderful to go up to the Christian Feast because the Jews also share the Feast and also talk excitedly about the coming of the Messiah. We join in that as Christians. We only tell them that he has been once already. But he is coming back at the Feast. I believe he will come back at the Feast of Tabernacles, to fulfil that Feast as he fulfilled Passover and Pentecost. It is the feast of the final harvest, the final ingathering. It all fits beautifully.

So here we have a Jesus coming back to earth. Why? Not only is he coming back to earth himself but he is bringing with him everybody in heaven. Now that is an extraordinary fact. I have spoken at four funerals of my close relatives. One was my daughter. The next was my mother-in-law, and then my brother-in-law and sister. At each of the funerals I said, "They'll all be back on earth one day." The people looked at me as if I was teaching reincarnation! It is extraordinary. These are Christians. They have never been told about the resurrection of the body, which will happen here, not in heaven. We don't need a body up there but we will need one here. This is where we will get it when Jesus comes back.

If I die before Jesus gets back, I will have a great advantage: I will get a front seat at the big meeting, because the dead in Christ will rise first. So, they get the front seats. The biggest, noisiest Christian meeting is going to take place when we meet the Lord. There is no stadium on earth big enough to hold it, so it has got to be up in the air. I tell you if you don't like noisy meetings, don't come. There will be archangels shouting their heads off, trumpets blasting, and I shall be shouting "Hallelujah!"

On my grandfather's gravestone in England there is his name, "David Ledger Pawson", and then underneath it says, "What a meeting!" That is not out of the Bible, it is from an old Methodist hymnbook. But I know what it means. He is looking forward to the big and noisy meeting when the Christians gather together to greet the return of the Lord. I can't wait for it. Read my book *When Jesus Returns*. We have such an exciting future to tell other people about.

I believe Jesus is coming back to *reign*. Not to judge – that will come later. But I believe the scripture is clear that he is coming back to reign and we shall reign with him. I am what is called a classical pre-millennialist. The early Church had only one view of the future, up to and including Augustine's early ministry. It was that he is coming back to reign over the nations of the world and that then all the prophecies which we tend to dismiss as poetry and myth will come true.

The prophecies of nature: being transformed; the wolf lying down with the lamb; the lion eating straw like the ox, and the children playing with snakes—do you dismiss all that as poetry? I believe God meant what he said and that there will be a transformed nature when Jesus is reigning. The whole creation is travailing and groaning, waiting until what? Waiting for the redemption of our bodies. That is going to take place when he gets back and we get our new bodies on earth.

I love preaching about the resurrection of the body. In fact, I had the opportunity to preach on the resurrection of the body to a hundred old-age pensioners, which was very exciting. What kind of a body will I have? Well, it says it will be like his glorious body. So how old will I be when I get my new body? The answer is thirty-three, and when you are in your seventies and eighties you can't wait to be thirty-three again!

This is the truth. I am going to have a new body on earth, from Jesus, in a moment, in the twinkling of an eye. That is one for the creationist—a brand new body! Do you really believe that? I do, and I am excited about that. Especially when I am speaking to handicapped and crippled people, I love to tell them that they are going to get a new body. We shall reign with him.

Now that was the universal belief of the early Church. There was no debate. Then in Augustine's later ministry, he reacted and went back to his Greek education. It is a tragedy. He reacted against physical things. This was partly a reaction to his promiscuous life and his having an illegitimate son before he was a Christian, but it was also the Neo-Platonic teaching he had received when he was a student. He reacted against the thought of a physical return of Christ to a physical earth to reign over physical nations. From that day on, the Church never preached about the new earth again. It was replaced with a "going to heaven", which is a tragic loss. It is the Greek phobia about things physical.

You see, the Jews never had that. I like to tell people that I found a wonderful prayer in the Jewish prayer book to use when you go to the toilet. Isn't that lovely? You see, to us that is funny, but if I mention it to a Jewish audience, nobody smiles. They say, "But of course." The God of the Bible is as interested in what you do in the toilet as what you do in church. If you don't understand that, you haven't got hold of the biblical God yet, because he made the physical world. He is interested in our bodies and not just our souls. I have been in lots of Christian toilets as I stay with families, and they have a pile of devotional books there. They have texts up on the wall. Everything is designed to take your mind to heavenly things while you are in there—totally Greek and totally un-Hebrew. That prayer actually says, "Lord, I praise you that my body is working," and I've reached the age where that becomes quite a prayer of thanksgiving when your waterworks and bowels don't always do what they should. Then you praise the Lord that you feel better, and you come out having had a good "Hallelujah" in there.

Now to the Greek Western thinking, it is ludicrous that God should be like that. But you see he is concerned to save my body as well as my soul, because he made both. One day he is going to give me a new body to live in a new world eventually—a new earth. If you preach, when did you last preach about the new earth? Or do you just talk about people going to heaven? I ask people, "Do you want to live on the new earth?" I was preaching in Sydney, Australia, a few miles from Bondi Beach. I said, "In the new earth there will be no sun, no sea, and no sex." Nobody said, "Hallelujah." It was a deadly hush, and they all looked as if they wanted to get out and get down to Bondi Beach quickly, because you can get all three down at Bondi Beach. I said, "That new earth will be such a wonderful place that you won't miss any of those three things."

Do you preach about the new earth?—because that is going to be our new home and it is where God is going to live. The biggest surprise in the Bible is the last page where God says, "I'm going to live with you in the new earth" and God comes down as the New Jerusalem comes down out of heaven. In astonishment, the angel says, "Look, behold, the dwelling place of God is with men, and they will be his people and he shall be their God." We have got a hope for the future that nobody can match. Why are we not proclaiming it widely and saying, "You can share that hope, but you'll need to be prepared for that new earth, and you'll need a new body, and you can have all of it in Christ." What a hope we have got. I love preaching eschatological themes about the future. In a hopeless world, a despairing world, what a message it is.

So, my final point is: let us get back to the future, and let us get back to the Christian hope. Not only hope for an individual of going to heaven, but hope for the world, the hope that will bring peace. I went to the United Nations headquarters in New York once when I had about six hours between flights. I got a yellow taxi to take me to the UN building. There were two things I wanted to see.

The first is outside the entrance, in the grass. There is a big block of granite on which is inscribed half a verse of scripture. Talk about taking scripture out of context— this is a classic example. It says, "And they will beat their swords into ploughshares and their spears into pruning hooks; nation will not lift up sword against nation, neither shall they learn war anymore". But that is only half the verse. The first half says, "When the Lord reigns in Zion he will settle the disputes between the nations, and they will beat their swords". Multilateral disarmament can only come when Jesus is back and is reigning in Zion. So, they built the United Nations headquarters in the wrong place.

Well, I was shown around with a little group by a young lady in a blue uniform. She said, "This is the Security Council"; "This is the General Assembly"; "These are the committee rooms", and she took us all around. Then, after two hours, she said, "Well ladies and gentlemen, that ends our tour. Have a nice day."

I said, "But you haven't shown this one room."

"Which room?" she asked, and I described it.

"Oh no," she said, "that's locked up. You can't get in there; it's not open to the public."

"But," I said, "that's the room I came to see. I want to see in there. I've heard about it, and I can't believe what I've heard, and I must see it."

"No," she said, "I'm sorry. You can't."

I said, "I've come an awful long way to see it." Still she didn't give in. So I tried my last card and I said, "I've come all the way from little old England to see it." Now that really impresses the Americans. You really can reach their heart when you say, "I'm from little old England."

She said, "*I* can't let you in there, but go to the foyer and ask one of the guards if you can get in."

So I thought, "Well, we're winning." I went to the guard and said, "Could you please show me this room?"

He replied, "No it's closed to the public; it's locked up."

I continued, "But I'd like to see it."

"No, I'm sorry you can't."

"I've come a long way."

"Well."

"I've come all the way from little old England."

Then he said, "How long do you want to be in there?"

"Two minutes."

"Oh, if it's just two minutes....." He got a key, walked across the foyer, opened the door, and let me in.

Then I saw the god of the United Nations, to whom they pray for world peace. It is a dark room, of modest size. No windows. There is a bit of light around the edge of the ceilings, so it is very dim and very dark. There is a circle of prayer mats and stools for people to kneel or sit and pray, and in the middle is the god. It is a big black block of cast iron, the size and shape of a coffin, on a pedestal. They kneel down and pray to this big black block for world peace. Now I had been told about this and I couldn't believe what I had been told. But I have seen it with my own eyes.

What happened was this. When the UN headquarters was built, Dag Hammarskjöld from Sweden said, "We've no prayer room, and we ought to have a room for meditation." So they built this extra room between two wings. That is why it has no windows. Then they had a huge debate over what to put in the room. Americans wanted a cross, but that was ruled out. Then the Hindus wanted flowers, and that was ruled out. Then the Muslims wanted something else. So finally, they approached a famous sculptor and said, "Will you please make a sculpture that represents all the gods of the world, in which each person can see their own god." So the sculptor made this big block and painted it a matte black paint so that there is no reflection. You kneel down, you look into this blackness and you see your god, and you pray. This big black block is to represent all the gods. Therefore, it is shapeless. It is black. It is nothing, and you are looking into nothing when you pray to it. I said, "Now I've seen it."

I could have wept. To think that praying to a big black block in New York is going to bring world peace and cause everybody to beat their swords into ploughshares and their spears into pruning hooks is crazy. But my hope is that one day that half verse will be fulfilled, when the other half has come true, and when the return of Christ happens, during which he will reign over the nations. When I go to Australia I say, "You will never be a republic. You already have a King, and he's Jewish." Norway has a Jewish King: Jesus. One day he will return to reign over the nations, and he will settle the disputes between the nations with total righteousness and justice. When there is total justice there can be total peace, because the lack of peace is always due to some sense of injustice. That is my hope for the future: Jesus coming back.

I will tell you frankly that in England there are more Christians pinning their hopes to revival than to the return of Christ. That grieves me. The centre of our hope for the future is Christ's second visit to planet earth. "Maranatha," has been the cry of the Church from the first century, even keeping the language in which that prayer was first offered, "Even so, come Lord Jesus."

What I have been trying to do is to paint a picture of the twenty-first century Church that God is looking for. My big question is: will he get it? Where will reformation come from? Will it come from the top or the bottom? Occasionally it has come from the top. John XXIII, that amazing old man they thought they had put in as a caretaker until the next one was ready, prayed every day for two things. He prayed for a new Pentecost and he prayed for Israel. Very few people know that, but I got that from his chaplain. These were his two great concerns, that there would be a new Pentecost, a new outpouring of the Spirit on the Catholic Church, and he prayed for Israel, that the Church and Israel will be reconciled. So, Vatican II, which changed so much, did come from the top, quite unexpectedly to most. But I have to say that reformation, although it occasionally comes from the top, usually comes from the bottom as unknown nobodies stand for the truth and face whatever cost there may be.

Luther was from the bottom. He was just a simple monk and not very noticed, except for his terrible introverted self-examination and self-flagellation. Who would have taken notice of that man? But God took that nobody and made him a somebody. I believe this reformation, which I long to see, which I have spelled out for you, will come from the bottom, from ordinary people in the pews. I find some of them way ahead of their own leaders in their understanding of where the Church should go.

So I am looking for the Jan Hus, the Martin Luther, the John Brown, the nobodies who will start standing absolutely firmly on the Word of God, saying, "Here I stand. My conscience is bound to the Word of God. I can do no other." The more ordinary Christians who will do that and say, "We're just not going to be tied to tradition; we're not going to be tied to politicians; we're going to be tied to the Lord Jesus Christ and his Word, and by the power of the Holy Spirit, make a difference" the better.

I believe reformation will come from the bottom. Where will resistance come to such a reformation? From inside the Church or outside? Well, some will come from outside, from politicians, particularly from the left-wing who are increasingly liberal and anti-Christian. But I believe the major opposition to reformation always comes from the inside of the Church. That is painful. It comes from the officials of the Church who stand for the status quo and against rocking the boat. I believe there will be terrific opposition from ecclesiastical authorities to any reformation of the Church. So it is painful.

I think you will understand if I say that the two painful things that I experienced in my ministry are: first, church leaders who seem blind and deaf, who don't even see any threat in Islam, who are just happy and content even with declining congregations; but second, and this has been the greatest pain that I experienced, and I am being very frank here, is from Christians and church leaders who agree with me but will not stand publicly with me. I have encountered so many of them. They say, "Oh David, thank you. Thank God for what you're saying." I reply, "Well, will you please say it with me? I could do with somebody on the platform with me from time to time." People have said (literally) to me, "I could do with that like a hole in the head."

It really is tragic that there are Christians who know when they hear the truth and who agree with it privately, but dare not risk going public. If only all those who agree with this reformation actually did something.... That is the tragedy. I believe we could do this if all those who really believe the truth would come out with it and stand firm, even if it cost them their job and their house.

I have told you it cost us that, but we have never regretted it and the Lord has kept his promise to look after us ever since. One week after we lost our house we were presented with a brand-new house that had never been lived in, and I had a church to minister to. The Lord is good. But he had to take me to that point where I had to say, "I'm prepared to risk everything rather than go against my conscience." I believe he calls us all to do that. But it is costly, and the fear of people can be a real factor in holding you back. But I believe if you fear God you will never fear anybody or anything else.

www.ingramcontent.com/pod-product-compliance
Lightning Source LLC
Chambersburg PA
CBHW071022080526
44587CB00015B/2453